Briefly:
Ayer's *Language, Truth and Logic*

The SCM *Briefly* series

Briefly: Ayer's
Language, Truth and Logic

David Mills Daniel

scm press

The Author has asserted his right under the Copyright, Designs and
Patents Act, 1988, to be identified as the Author of this Work

The author and publisher acknowledge material reproduced from A. J.
Ayer, *Language, Truth and Logic*, reprinted with an Introduction by Ben
Rogers, London: Penguin Books, 2001, ISBN 0141186046. The material
from A. J. Ayer's *Language, Truth and Logic* is reproduced by permission
of Victor Gollancz, an imprint of The Orion Publishing Group.

British Library Cataloguing in Publication data

A catalogue record for this book is available
from the British Library

978 0 334 04122 1

First published in 2007 by SCM Press
13–17 Long Lane,
London ECIA 9PN

www.scm-canterburypress.co.uk

SCM Press is a division of
SCM-Canterbury Press Ltd

Typeset by Regent Typesetting, London
Printed and bound in Great Britain by
CPI Bookmarque Ltd, Croydon, Surrey

Contents

Contents

Introduction

The SCM *Briefly* series, edited by David Mills Daniel, is designed to enable students and general readers to acquire knowledge and understanding of key texts in philosophy, philosophy of religion, theology and ethics. While the series will be especially helpful to those following university and A-level courses in philosophy, ethics and religious studies, it will in fact be of interest to anyone looking for a short guide to the ideas of a particular philosopher or theologian.

Each book in the series takes a piece of work by one philosopher and provides a summary of the original text, which adheres closely to it, and contains direct quotations from it, thus enabling the reader to follow each development in the philosopher's argument(s). Throughout the summary, there are page references to the original philosophical writing, so that the reader has ready access to the primary text. In the Introduction to each book, you will find details of the edition of the philosophical work referred to.

In *Briefly: Ayer's Language, Truth and Logic*, we refer to A. J. Ayer, *Language, Truth and Logic* (reprinted with an Introduction by Ben Rogers), London: Penguin Books, 2001, ISBN 0141186046.

Each *Briefly* begins with an Introduction, followed by a chapter on the Context in which the work was written. Who was this writer? Why was this book written? With Some Issues to Consider, and some Suggestions for Further Reading, this *Briefly* aims to get anyone started in their philosophical investigation. The Detailed Summary of the philosophical work is followed by a concise chapter-by-chapter Overview and an extensive Glossary of terms.

Bold type is used in the Detailed Summary and Overview sections to indicate the first occurrence of words and phrases that appear in the Glossary. The Glossary also contains terms used elsewhere in this *Briefly* guide and other terms that readers may encounter in their study of Ayer's *Language, Truth and Logic*.

Context

Who was A. J. Ayer?

Alfred Jules Ayer was born in London in 1910. He was a King's Scholar at Eton, and won a scholarship to Christ Church, Oxford, where he gained a first in 'Greats' (Greek and Ancient philosophy). After studying at the University of Vienna, where he got to know the leading logical positivists of the Vienna Circle, such as Moritz Schlick, Rudolf Carnap and Friedrich Waismann, Ayer lectured in philosophy at Christ Church, where he was elected to a research studentship (fellowship) in 1935. In 1940 he joined the Welsh Guards, serving in the Special Operations Executive (SOE) and as an attaché at the British Embassy in Paris. After a year as fellow and dean of Wadham College, Oxford, Ayer became Grote Professor of the Philosophy of Mind and Logic at University College, London in 1946, and was Wykeham Professor of Logic at Oxford (and a fellow of New College) from 1959 to 1978.

Ayer's approach to philosophy was influenced by the work of Bertrand Russell, G. E. Moore, Ludwig Wittgenstein, the logical positivists of the Vienna Circle, and, in particular, the empiricism of David Hume. *Language, Truth and Logic* (published in 1936), a robust statement of Ayer's version of logical positivism and of the view that philosophy should confine itself to analysis, and avoid metaphysical and theological

speculation, had an immediate impact and was highly controversial. Ayer's other books include *The Foundations of Empirical Knowledge* (1940), *The Problem of Knowledge* (1956), *Philosophical Essays* (1954) and *Russell and Moore: The Analytical
Heritage* (1971).

Outside philosophy, Ayer was interested in a wide range of
social and political issues. In the 1930s, he stood as a Labour
candidate for Westminster Council, and served as President
of both the British Humanist Association and the Homo-
sexual Law (later Sexual Law) Reform Society, which helped
to secure the passing of the 1967 Sexual Offences Act. He
was a member of the Central Advisory Council for Education
(England), which produced the Plowden Report on primary
education. Ayer was knighted in 1970, and died in 1989.

What is *Language, Truth and Logic*?

As Ayer acknowledges in the Appendix he wrote for the re-
publication of *Language, Truth and Logic* in 1946, he was a
young man when it first appeared, and it was written with
'more passion' than most works of philosophy. For Ayer had a
mission: under influences which included the logical positivism of the Vienna Circle, Hume and Russell's 'empiricism'
(the philosophical view, shared by Ayer, that experience is the
(only) source of knowledge) and Moore's 'analytical approach',
he wished to carry out the 'trial and execution of metaphysics, using the verification principle', and to make it clear that
philosophy could only contribute to knowledge, if it confined
itself to the 'practice of analysis' (Ayer, *Part of My Life*).

Ayer does not waste time on preliminaries. Chapter 1 is entitled 'The Elimination of Metaphysics', in which he argues
that philosophy's role does not include the metaphysical one

of trying to attain knowledge of a world that transcends those of science and common sense, in order to discover the nature of ultimate reality. Indeed, the metaphysician's claim to have access to facts that cannot be known from sense-experience is excluded by the rule determining language's literal significance. A sentence can only express a genuine proposition about a matter of fact, if it is empirically verifiable: that is, if it is known what observations are relevant to determining whether it is true or false. Ayer gives the example of a supposed metaphysical proposition from the idealist philosopher F. H. Bradley's *Appearance and Reality*: 'the Absolute enters into, but is itself incapable of, evolution and progress'. Although this sentence has a similar grammatical structure to, 'The man enters the house through the door, but is incapable of getting in by the window', the all-important difference between them is that no observations are relevant to determining the truth or falsehood of the first, whereas it is obvious what observations we would make to decide the truth of the second. Bradley's supposed proposition is not empirically verifiable, and is, therefore, a metaphysical pseudo-proposition.

Ayer spells out exactly what he means by verifiability. There are propositions about matters of fact, which there are no known practical means of verifying, but they are significant, because it is known what observations would determine their truth, so they are verifiable in principle. It is also important to distinguish between strong and weak senses of verifiability. The first refers to conclusive verifiability, advocated by some logical positivists, but rejected by Ayer. Such general propositions as 'all men are mortal' cannot be conclusively verified by any finite series of observations, so adopting conclusive verifiability as the criterion of significance would mean treating them like metaphysical statements. He prefers a weaker form

3

of the verification principle: a proposition is genuinely factual, if any observations are relevant to determining its truth or falsehood. Thus, the supposed propositions of monists, who say reality is one substance, and pluralists, who say it is many, are both nonsensical. This does not mean that they are incomprehensible gibberish (in the 1946 Appendix, Ayer concedes that 'meaning' is used in a 'variety of senses', and statements that are not empirically verifiable may be 'meaningful' in some sense), but that, as no possible observations are relevant to determining whether or not they are true, they lack factual content, and so are not literally meaningful. The only other literally meaningful propositions are the *a priori* ones of logic and pure mathematics, the truth of which can be determined analytically. Ayer emphasizes the nature and purpose of factual propositions: they are empirical hypotheses, which provide a rule for anticipating experience, so some actual or possible experience must be relevant to them.

How does metaphysics occur? Ayer explains how it arises from ambiguities and imprecision in language. A thing's sensible properties can only be referred to in language that seems to stand for the thing itself, as distinct from what is said about it. Those who believe that there must be a single real entity, corresponding to every name, then think that there is a 'thing itself', distinct from the sensible properties, and the term 'substance' is applied to it. Sentences that express existential propositions can be confusing. 'Martyrs exist' has the same grammatical form as 'martyrs suffer' (a noun followed by an intransitive verb), so may also be thought to attribute a property to them. It is said that, to be fictitious, such creatures as unicorns must exist, but that, as it is self-contradictory to maintain that fictitious objects exist, they exist in some special, non-empirical sense. Ayer does not accuse metaphysicians of intending to write nonsense: they are deceived into it by grammar or reasoning errors. He does not deny that some metaphysical writings may express genuine mystical feeling, but they are not literally meaningful and so are not part of philosophy.

Abandoning metaphysics (Chapter 2) frees philosophy from trying to build a deductive system of first principles, which gives a complete picture of reality. Philosophical system-builders, like the rationalist philosopher (one who believes that reason is the principal source of knowledge) Descartes, had tried to find a secure base for all knowledge in logically certain *a priori* principles (the truth of which is known independently of experience), such as his 'I think, therefore I am', which it would be self-contradictory to deny, rather than in inductive ones (those verified by experience). But, quite apart from the fact that a thought occurring at a particular time does not entail a series, sufficient to constitute a single self, *a priori* principles cannot be the source of the whole truth about the universe: they are logically certain, only because they are tautologies (the concept of their subject includes that of their predicate), so only further tautologies can be validly deduced from them.

For Ayer, philosophy's function is modest. Not only does it not include providing a complete picture of reality, or an absolutely secure base for knowledge, it does not even involve testing the validity of scientific hypotheses or everyday assumptions. As empirical verification is the only possible justification for any kind of empirical proposition, science does not need to wait until philosophers have solved the so-called problem of induction: that is, identified a means of proving that empirical generalizations, based on past experience, will apply in the future. And, if it did, it would be a long wait, as the two ways of tackling the problem cannot solve it. Trying to deduce the principle of induction from an *a priori* principle would make the mistake of trying to deduce a proposition about a matter of fact from a tautology. However, trying to deduce it from an empirical principle would involve assuming the truth of what needs to be proved: induction cannot be justified on the grounds of the uniformity of nature, as this assumes the reliability of past experience as a guide to the future. In fact (Ayer contends), the problem of induction is not a real problem. Induction does not need a philosophical justification: the only relevant test of it is that it works, and enables us to anticipate the future. It is the same with the so-called problem of perception. Philosophers, interested in epistemology, think that belief in material things is unjustified without a satisfactory analysis of perception. But what justifies this common sense belief is our having sensations: sense-experience is the sole basis of the validity of perceptual judgements.

As Ayer has radically revised the philosopher's job description, and removed so many major items from it, what is left? The answer is analysis. This does not make any metaphysical or empirical assumptions about the nature of things, nor, when he analyses facts and notions, is the philosopher undertaking any metaphysical or empirical enquiry: his concern is with the definitions of the corresponding words. His task, by exposing the logical complexity of sentences, and clarifying their meaning, is to facilitate scientific enquiry and ordinary discourse, and to remove the confusions that give rise to metaphysics. Ayer contends that the history of philosophy shows that the great philosophers, from Plato to Kant, and from Locke and Hume to Mill, were analysts, not metaphysicians; but even if no philosophers fitted his definition, it would still be correct.

Ayer uses Russell's theory of descriptions to explain (Chapter 3) how philosophical analysis works. Its concern is not with explicit definitions of the kind found in dictionaries, which provide a synonym for a word or phrase (symbol(s)), but with definitions in use, which clarify meaning, and eliminate (metaphysical) confusions, by showing how a sentence(s), in which a particular word or phrase (symbol(s)) occurs, can be translated into one(s) that does not, but which shows that only one object, or no object, possesses a certain property. Ayer uses the examples of 'The round square cannot exist' and 'The author of *Waverley* was Scotch'. The first becomes, 'No one thing can be both square and round'. This shows how to eliminate any definite descriptive phrase that occurs as the subject of a negative existential sentence, making it plain that no such object as a round square can exist (it is not an object that exists in some special, non-empirical sense). The second becomes, 'One person, and one person only, wrote *Waverley*, and that person was Scotch', exposing the statement's meaning, and demonstrating that it can apply to only one person.

Ayer points out that one of the principal elements in the problem of perception is devising a rule for translating sentences about material things into ones about sense-contents (the term Ayer prefers to sense-data, to describe what is immediately known in sensation, as opposed to the material objects, which are believed to be their source). When we talk about material things, we are referring to logical constructions (when something is defined logically in terms of something else) out of our sense-contents, and showing the principles of this construction (as Ayer attempts to do in this chapter) indicates their relationship. The mistake philosophers make (he maintains), when trying to describe the nature of material things, is to think that they are dealing with a factual question about the properties of things, not one about definitions and the relationship of symbols standing for sense-contents. Through not being aware of the logical complexity of a sentence like 'This is a table', they may adopt a metaphysical belief about the existence of material substances.

Empirical generalizations can be verified in experience many times, but never be logically certain, as they could be confuted in the future. But how, without accepting the rationalists' view that there are truths known independently of experience, does an empiricist account for logical and mathematical truths, which seem to be necessary and certain? There are only (Chapter 4) two possibilities: to deny that they are necessary and certain, or to accept that they lack factual content. Mill (Ayer explains) adopted the first alternative, arguing that logical and mathematical truths are inductive generalizations, based on very many supporting instances, but differing from scientific hypotheses, not in kind, but in degree of probability. Ayer considers Mill's view to be incompatible with the way we regard such truths. He gives the example of counting what are thought to be five pairs of objects, but finding that there are only nine objects. Nobody thinks the disparity has arisen because two times five is no longer ten; it is put down to counting errors. And this is what happens whenever mathematical or logical truths seem in doubt; we preserve their validity by finding another explanation.

Thus, there is no mystery about the absolute certainty of logical and mathematical propositions. They are analytic propositions or tautologies, which are universally true, because they are not allowed to be anything else. Unlike synthetic propositions (ones that give factual information; Ayer does not agree with Kant that mathematical propositions are synthetic), the validity of analytic propositions is not decided by experience, but depends entirely on the definitions of the symbols they contain. They express our determination to make the symbols used in them synonymous, so denying them is self-contradictory: asserting that two times two is not four breaches the logical law of non-contradiction. Experience cannot confute them, because they give no information about a matter of fact. However, unlike metaphysical utterances, they are literally meaningful, because they clarify the use of certain symbols. But, if they consist of analytic propositions, why are mathematics and logic still interesting and surprising, and how do errors arise in them? Ayer explains that it is due to the limitations of the human intellect. A being whose intellect was infinitely powerful would see all the possible implications of the definitions used immediately, and not make any mistakes.

Before (Chapter 5) discussing how empirical or synthetic propositions are validated, Ayer deals with the question of why his theory of truth only addresses the issue of how propositions are validated, not the metaphysical question of the nature of truth itself. It is because to enquire about truth is just to ask whether a particular proposition is true or false. The statement, 'It is true that Queen Anne is dead', just states, 'Queen Anne is dead'; the 'is true' is logically superfluous, merely signifying assertion. However, philosophers are beguiled into a metaphysical view of truth, because the grammatical form of sentences in which the word 'truth' appears suggests that it stands for some metaphysical entity.

But how are empirical propositions validated? The criterion for deciding the validity of analytic propositions is inadequate for determining that of synthetic ones, which can be false, even if not self-contradictory. They are all hypotheses, the truth of which is verified (or their falsehood determined)

9

by actual sense-experience. Ayer explains how the process works. Generally, empirical hypotheses, such as scientific laws, do not exist in isolation; they are part of a system of hypotheses, which explain aspects of our environment or experience, and enable us to anticipate the future. Just as confirmatory observations do not make these hypotheses logically certain, unfavourable ones do not force us to relinquish them. We may conclude that the conditions were different from those in which the law's operation has been observed. However, though cherished hypotheses can be retained in the face of contrary observations, the possibility of their being relinquished must exist, otherwise they cease to be genuine hypotheses: the possibility of their being invalidated by experience must be accepted.

Indeed, unless contrary observations are accepted, and changes (including radical ones) made to our accepted system of hypotheses, it will cease to function as an accurate predictor of the future. If experience has indicated that it contains flaws, it will probably continue to fail, until it is modified. To say that confirmatory observations increase a hypothesis' probability (or those of a system) does not refer to an intrinsic property of the hypothesis, but indicates the increased degree of confidence that it is rational to place in it.

One of the most controversial aspects of *Language, Truth and Logic* is Ayer's treatment (Chapter 6) of moral and religious issues, as he rejects the view that there can be two kinds of speculative knowledge: of empirical fact and questions of value (ethics and aesthetics). He accepts that for some moralists, such as subjectivists, who define goodness and rightness in terms of feelings of approval, and utilitarians, who define them in terms of pleasure or happiness, and who both commit what Moore labelled the 'naturalistic fallacy' (defining 'good' or right' in terms of a natural property), statements of ethical value can be translated into statements of empirical fact: about whether the things in question are approved of or pleasant. However, although ethical symbols, such as 'good' and 'right', can be used purely descriptively (for example, to state society's disapproval of certain kinds of conduct), this is not how they are generally used: including by those moralists who commit the naturalistic fallacy. Most ethical statements are normative, expressing judgements of value and/or prescribing conduct. As it is always (again a point made by Moore) an open question (it can be asked intelligibly) whether anything that is said to be good actually is, ethical statements cannot be reduced to non-ethical ones. It is certainly not self-contradictory to hold that things or actions which are generally approved of are not right or good, or to say that performing the action, which would probably produce the greatest happiness, is sometimes wrong.

For Ayer, ethical statements are not literally meaningful, because they just express emotions. He gives the example of a statement about stealing money. Adding an ethical symbol like 'wrong' to it adds (he maintains) nothing to the statement's factual content; it only expresses moral disapproval of the action, and cannot be true or false. In fact, Ayer espouses an emotivist theory of ethics: that ethical terms have the purely emotive function of expressing and arousing feelings, stimulating action, and functioning as commands. He notes Moore's contention that ethical statements cannot just be about feelings, as questions of value are disputed, but denies that such disputes are about moral values, as opposed to the motives for, and effects of, actions. Participants in ethical disputes hope that securing their opponents' agreement about the facts will change their moral feelings.

Ayer identifies the major causes of moral behaviour and debate as fear of God's displeasure and society's disapproval. This is why moral precepts are often regarded as categorical commands, and moral sanctions are invoked to promote or prevent behaviour that increases or diminishes society's well-being. However, there is no objective way to determine the validity of any ethical system or principles; and, instead of attempting to do so, moral philosophy should confine itself to what we would call 'metaethics': studying the meaning and use of such moral terms as 'good' and 'right' and the nature of moral argument.

But, even if we agree with Ayer that normative ethical statements are not ordinary empirical propositions, and accept that ethical terms (often) have an emotive function, his account does not seem to do justice to (the complexity of) ethics and ethical debate. To take Ayer's example, an ethical dispute may well involve facts, but will not be confined to them. It could involve disagreement about the facts of a particular situation; then, given such disagreement, given different opinions about which course of action would be most likely to maximize happiness; and, finally, different views about whether or not happiness is the ultimate good. Again, those who take the view that morality is grounded in the needs of intrinsically valuable human beings would probably regard the statement that murder or torture is wrong as clearly true.

Ayer is equally dismissive of the possibility of religious knowledge. So, far from God's existence being demonstratively certain, as some religious people believe, it is not even probable. 'God' is a metaphysical term, and no metaphysical utterance can be either true or false. The word 'God' fosters the illusion that a real entity corresponds to it, but it is not a genuine name; while saying that human beings have a soul, which survives death, is another metaphysical assertion that lacks factual content. But, although Ayer is right to point out that religious statements about God's existence and attributes are not ordinary empirical propositions, like those about the existence or attributes of human beings, and cannot be verified by sense-experience, the concepts they contain are intelligible, and can be argued for, and about, rationally. Anselm's version of the ontological argument and Aquinas' cosmological argument may not work as objective proofs of God's existence, but they are cogent statements of the theistic case, which draw attention to important features of the concept of God and/or different ways of understanding the universe. They need to be refuted in detail, as they were by Hume and Kant; it is not enough just to sweep them aside as 'metaphysical utterances'.

In his discussion of our knowledge of the self and others (Chapter 7), Ayer again emphasizes that empirical knowledge does not require a basis of certainty: unless there are metaphysical objects (which he holds there are not), sense-experience is our only source of knowledge, and this empirical knowledge lacks logical certainty. As far as the self is concerned, a phenomenalist standpoint has to be adopted: it is legitimate to say that a particular subject experiences a given sense-content(s), but this has to be understood not, as Descartes maintained, in terms of a metaphysical 'substantival ego' (the mind or self as a pure, indivisible and imperishable substance), but in terms of the relationship between sense-contents. A metaphysical self is not disclosed in self-consciousness; cannot be located anywhere; and is unverifiable. As Hume had pointed out, there are only perceptions (sense-contents), leading him to conclude that the self is a mere bundle of different perceptions, lacking any clear unifying principle: while self-consciousness has to be defined in terms of memory, self-identity cannot be, as perceptions that are not recalled constitute the self as much as those that are. Hume's inability to identify a unifying principle had resulted in rationalist philosophers criticizing empiricist accounts of the self as inadequate, but the problem can be solved (Ayer believes) by defining personal identity in terms of bodily identity, and the latter in terms of the resemblance and continuity of sense-contents. This definition of personal identity is borne out by the fact that it is not self-contradictory to talk of an individual surviving memory loss, but it is of his surviving bodily annihilation. Hume's mistake had been to conceive of the self as an aggregate of sense-experiences, not as reducible to them: to refer to the self is to refer to sense-experiences.

But does such thoroughgoing phenomenalism, and acceptance that sense-experiences are private to the self, mean that there is no reason for believing in the existence of others, leading to a solipsistic position? Ayer does not think so. It is wrong to hold that others' experiences are inaccessible. Just as material things and the self are defined in terms of their empirical manifestations, so are other people, in terms of their bodily behaviour. The hypothesis that others exist is verified by the appropriate series of sense-contents occurring, so the solution to the philosophical problem of knowledge of other people is to indicate the way that a certain type of hypothesis can be empirically verified. Thus, despite the private nature of individual experiences, we are entitled to hold that we inhabit a common world with others. However, while we may not require evidence, other than sense-experience, to convince us of the existence of other people, Ayer's analysis of the self does not seem to solve the problem of personal identity, or explain what constitutes the 'I' that continues through time.

In the concluding chapter (Chapter 8), Ayer addresses three of the principal controversies (those between rationalists and empiricists, realists and idealists, and monists and pluralists) to show that, as philosophy's role is analysis, not metaphysical speculation and system-building, there is no justification for the existence of different philosophical schools.

Ayer dismisses the rationalist view that there is a supra-sensible world, known by intellectual intuition, which alone is wholly real, as a senseless doctrine, for no empirical observation is relevant to it. Further, rationalists are wrong to hold that necessarily valid *a priori* propositions are speculative truths of reason. However, empiricists, who hold that all significant hypotheses are empirical, are also wrong. Necessarily valid *a priori* propositions are tautologies, and rejecting metaphysics does not involve denial that there are necessary truths. The positivist's criterion of conclusive verifiability for distinguishing between a metaphysical utterance and a genuine synthetic proposition must be rejected, as no synthetic proposition can be more than (highly) probable: a proposition is genuinely factual, if any empirical observations are relevant to its truth or falsehood.

Ayer considers the realist-idealist controversy to be metaphysical, because it concerns the issue of whether or not things have completely undetectable properties, so no observation can resolve it. The idealist philosopher George Berkeley had argued that material things cannot exist unperceived, because they are no more than their sensible qualities, which it would be self-contradictory to say exist unsensed. But Berkeley had misunderstood the relationship between material things and the sense-contents that constitute them. Sense-contents are not parts of material things. The latter are logical constructions from the former; and this is a linguistic proposition: that to say anything about the first is equivalent to saying something about the second. A material thing can exist, without being sensed, if it is capable of being sensed and is a permanent possibility of sensation: material things are to be defined in terms of the hypothetical occurrence of sense-contents. Further, the fact that one perceives a table and other objects, one has always done so, and has seen others doing so, is a good inductive basis for the generalization that, in certain conditions, they are always perceptible, even when no one actually perceives them. Thus, material things can exist unperceived.

Ayer defines monists as believing that stating any fact about a thing is to state every fact about everything, such that any true proposition can be deduced from any other, from which it follows that any two sentences expressing true propositions are equivalent. As monists use 'truth' and 'reality' interchangeably, this leads to the metaphysical assertion that 'Reality is One'. He believes that their paradoxical conclusions arise from a crucial, false step in their argument: that all a thing's properties, including relational ones, are constitutive of its nature, which amounts to saying that they are defining properties of it. But to attribute to something a property that belongs to it by definition is to state a tautology: if all a thing's properties were constitutive of its nature, the absurd result would be that no synthetic fact could be stated about it. Monists also maintain that every event is causally connected with every other. But causality is not a logical relation; if it were, the contradictory of every true proposition, stating a causal connection, would be self-contradictory, which is not the case. It would also make all data relevant to every scientific prediction, ruling out the possibility of making any. Thus, the monist doctrine is wrong.

Ayer concludes by summing up the role of philosophy and the philosopher. It is to become the logic of science, elucidating scientific theory, by defining its symbols, and making clear the logical relationship between scientific hypotheses, and (not, in Ayer's view, a difficult task) to analyse, and remove metaphysical confusions from, everyday language. To perform the first, and more important task, the philosopher must understand science.

Language, Truth and Logic is a robust and persuasive statement of the case for empiricism, the literal meaningfulness of only analytic and empirically verifiable propositions, and for regarding analysis as philosophy's (principal) role. And even those who do not accept that metaphysical propositions are pseudo-propositions must accept that they are not ordinary empirical propositions, the truth or falsehood of which can be determined by sense-experience. It is important, too, not to be disconcerted by the term 'literally meaningful'. This does not mean that metaphysical propositions are incomprehensible gibberish (if they were, they could not be discussed at all), but indicates that, unlike analytic and empirically verifiable propositions, there is no obvious or accepted means of deciding whether they are true or false. What is really controversial and disputable is Ayer's view that the whole of metaphysics, all of moral philosophy, apart from metaethics, and the philosophy of religion are not part of philosophy. The fact that the truth or falsehood of such propositions as, 'The soul is an indestructible and imperishable substance which survives physical death', 'A loving God created the universe', or, 'Actions are only right to the extent that they promote happiness', is not empirically verifiable does not mean that they cannot be rationally debated; and they relate to (philosophical) questions which human beings regard (and have always regarded) as being of fundamental importance. And who is (or should be) better equipped to make a constructive contribution to debate about them than the analytical philosopher?

Some Issues to Consider

- Ayer argues that philosophy's role does not include the metaphysical one of attaining knowledge of a world that transcends those of science and common sense, in order to discover the nature of ultimate reality.
- Ayer maintains that a sentence can only express a genuine proposition about a matter of fact if it is verifiable: that is, if it is known what observations are relevant to determining its truth or falsehood.
- As general propositions, such as 'All men are mortal', cannot be established with certainty by any finite series of observations, Ayer prefers a weaker form of the verification principle: adopting conclusive verifiability as the criterion of significance would mean treating general propositions like metaphysical statements.
- Metaphysical statements are not incomprehensible gibberish: they are 'nonsensical' in that, as no possible observations are relevant to determining their truth or falsehood, they lack factual content, while they are not *a priori* propositions either.
- Ayer believes metaphysics arises from ambiguities and imprecision in language. Do you agree?
- Do you agree with Ayer that philosophy is unable to solve the problem of induction, but that there is no need to solve it anyway, and that the only relevant test of it is that it works?
- According to Ayer, what justifies our common sense belief in material things is that we have sensations: sense-

experience is the sole basis of the validity of perceptual judgements.

- Ayer holds that the philosopher's task is analysis: by exposing the logical complexity of the sentences, in which facts and notions are expressed, he can clarify their meaning, facilitate scientific enquiry and ordinary discourse, and remove the confusions that give rise to metaphysics.

- Philosophical analysis is concerned with definitions: not the explicit definitions, found in dictionaries, which provide a synonym for a word or phrase (symbol(s)), but definitions in use.

- These show how a sentence(s) in which a word or phrase (symbol(s)) occurs can be translated into one(s) that does not, but which shows that only one object, or no object, possesses a certain property.

- For example, 'The round square cannot exist' becomes 'No one thing can be both square and round', showing how to eliminate any definite descriptive phrase that occurs as the subject of a negative existential sentence, making it plain that no such object as a round square can exist, so it is not an object that exists in some special, non-empirical sense.

- Material things are logical constructions out of sense-contents, and, when we talk about material things, we are referring to these; thus, one of the principal elements in the problem of perception is devising a rule for translating sentences about material things into ones about sense-contents.

- By being unaware of the logical complexity of a sentence, such as 'This is a table', philosophers may adopt a metaphysical belief about the existence of material substances.

- According to Ayer, logical and mathematical propositions are absolutely certain, because they are analytic propositions (ones in which the concept of the subject contains that of the predicate), which are universally true, because they are not allowed to be anything else.

- They express our determination to make the symbols used in them synonymous, so denying them is self-contradictory: asserting that two times two is not four breaches the logical law of non-contradiction.

- Ayer maintains that, despite being analytical, mathematical and logical propositions can still be interesting and surprising, and errors can arise in them, due to the limitations of the human intellect. Do you think he is right?

- Ayer believes that philosophers are beguiled into a metaphysical view of truth, because the grammatical form of sentences, in which the word 'truth' appears, suggests that it stands for some metaphysical entity.

- For Ayer, empirical propositions are all hypotheses, the truth of which is verified, or their falsehood determined, by actual sense-experience.

- Generally, empirical hypotheses, such as scientific laws, do not exist in isolation, but are part of a system of hypotheses, which explain aspects of our environment or experience, and enable us to anticipate the future.

- Ayer warns that, unless we accept the possibility that empirical hypotheses may be invalidated by experience, and make changes (including radical ones) to our accepted system of hypotheses, in line with observations that are contrary to it, it will cease to function as an accurate predictor of the future.

- For Ayer, normative ethical concepts cannot be reduced to empirical ones, because they are unanalysable pseudo-concepts: adding an ethical symbol to a statement adds nothing to its factual content, but only expresses moral disapproval of the action concerned, and cannot be true or false. Do you agree?

- Ayer adopts an emotivist theory of ethics: that ethical terms have the purely emotive function of expressing and arousing feelings, stimulating action, and functioning as commands.

- He also thinks that there is no objective way of determining the validity of any ethical system or principles, so moral philosophy should confine itself to metaethics: studying the meaning and use of such moral terms as 'good' and 'right' and the nature of moral argument.

- Ayer maintains that we cannot say it is even probable that God exists, as 'God' is a metaphysical term, and no metaphysical utterance can be either true or false. Is Ayer right to be so dismissive of the possibility of religious knowledge?

- Ayer holds that, in relation to the self, a phenomenalist standpoint has to be adopted: it is legitimate to say that a particular subject experiences a given sense-content(s), but this has to be understood, not in terms of a metaphysical substantival ego, but in terms of the relationship between sense-contents.

- He thinks it is wrong to hold that others' experiences are inaccessible: just as material things and the self are defined in terms of their empirical manifestations, so are other people, in terms of their bodily behaviour, so the hypothesis that others exist is verified by the appropriate series of sense-contents occurring.

- Ayer addresses three of the principal philosophical controversies (those between rationalists and empiricists, realists and idealists, and monists and pluralists) to show that, as philosophy's role is analysis, there is no justification for the existence of different philosophical schools.

- He thinks rationalists are wrong to hold that necessarily valid *a priori* propositions are speculative truths of reason; as are empiricists, who hold that all significant hypotheses are empirical: necessarily valid *a priori* propositions are tautologies.

- He argues that a material thing can exist, without being sensed, if it can be sensed and is a permanent possibility of sensation: material things are to be defined in terms of the hypothetical occurrence of sense-contents.

- He rejects the monist doctrine that any true proposition can be deduced from any other, and that every event is causally connected with every other.

- Do you agree with Ayer that philosophy's role is to become the logic of science, and to analyse, and remove metaphysical confusions from, everyday language?

Suggestions for Further Reading

A. J. Ayer, *Hume, A Very Short Introduction*, Oxford and New York: Oxford University Press, 2000.

A. J. Ayer, *Language, Truth and Logic* (reprinted with an Introduction by Ben Rogers), London: Penguin, 2001.

A. J. Ayer (ed.), *Logical Positivism*, London: Allen and Unwin, 1959.

A. J. Ayer, *Part of My Life*, London: William Collins, 1977.

A. J. Ayer, *Philosophical Essays*, London and New York: Macmillan, 1963.

A. J. Ayer, *Russell and Moore: The Analytical Heritage*, London and New York: Macmillan, 1973.

A. J. Ayer, *The Foundations of Empirical Knowledge*, London and New York: Macmillan, 1969.

Suggestions for Further Reading

A. J. Ayer, *The Problem of Knowledge*, London: Penguin, 1971.

G. Berkeley, *Three Dialogues between Hylas and Philonous*, new edition, Indianapolis/Cambridge: Hackett Publishing Company, 1988.

F. H. Bradley, *Appearance and Reality: A Metaphysical Essay*, Oxford: Oxford University Press, 1930.

R. Descartes, *Discourse on Method and Meditations on First Philosophy*, trans. D. A. Cress, fourth edition, Indianapolis/Cambridge: Hackett Publishing Company, 1998.

J. H. Hick, *Philosophy of Religion*, fourth edition, Englewood Cliffs, NJ: Prentice-Hall, 1990.

W. D. Hudson, *Modern Moral Philosophy*, London: Macmillan, 1970.

D. Hume, *An Enquiry Concerning Human Understanding*, ed. T. L. Beauchamp, Oxford: Oxford University Press, 1999.

D. Hume, *A Treatise of Human Nature*, ed. E. C. Mossner, London: Penguin, 1969.

I. Kant, *Critique of Pure Reason*, ed. V. Politis, London: Everyman, 1993.

G. MacDonald and C. Wright (eds), *Fact, Science and Morality: Essays on A. J. Ayer's 'Language Truth and Logic'*, Oxford: Oxford University Press, 1986.

G. E. Moore, *Philosophical Studies*, London: Routledge, 2000.

G. E. Moore, *Principia Ethica*, ed. T. Baldwin, revised edition, Cambridge: Cambridge University Press, 1993.

B. Rogers, *A. J. Ayer, A Life*, London: Chatto and Windus, 1999.

B. A. W. Russell, *Introduction to Mathematical Philosophy*, ed. J. Slater, London: Routledge, 1993.

B. A. W. Russell, *The Problems of Philosophy* (reissued second edition, with Introduction by John Skorupski), Oxford: Oxford University Press, 2001.

J. O. Urmson, *Philosophical Analysis*, Oxford: Clarendon Press, 1956.

G. J. Warnock, *English Philosophy Since 1900*, Oxford: Oxford University Press, 1969.

Detailed Summary of A. J. Ayer's
Language, Truth and Logic

Preface to First Edition (pp. 9–11)

The views expressed below derive from those of **Russell** and **Wittgenstein**, which are in turn the 'logical outcome' of **Berkeley** and **Hume**'s '**empiricism**' (p. 9). I follow the latter's division of 'genuine propositions' into what he calls '**relations of ideas**', comprising the '*a priori* **propositions**' of **logic** and pure mathematics', which are '**necessary** and certain', because they are '**analytic**' and say nothing about the '**empirical world**', and those concerning 'empirical matters of fact', which can be '**probable** but never certain' (p. 9). In explaining how these are validated, I have 'explained the nature of truth' (p. 9). I employ a '**modified verification principle**' to test whether a sentence 'expresses a genuine **empirical hypothesis**': it need not be '**conclusively verifiable**', but a 'possible **sense-experience**' must be 'relevant' to determining its 'truth or falsehood' (p. 9). If not, and it is not 'a **tautology**' either, it is '**metaphysical**', and so 'literally **senseless**' (p. 9). By this '**criterion**', much that is regarded as **philosophy**, such as the existence of a '**transcendent God**', or a '**non-empirical world of values**', turns out to be 'metaphysical' (pp. 9–10).

The **philosopher** cannot provide '**speculative truths**' that 'compete with the **hypotheses of science**', or make '*a priori* judgements' about the 'validity' of scientific theories: his role is to 'clarify' its propositions (p. 10). This removes any reason for '**conflicting philosophical "schools"**'; and I shall prove this by solving the 'problems' that have divided philosophers (p. 10). The view that 'philosophizing' is an **analytical activity** is 'associated' with '**Moore** and his disciples', but they do not share my 'thoroughgoing **phenomenalism**' (p. 10). My views are 'closest' to those of such '**logical positivists**' as **Schlick** and **Carnap** (p. 10). I am also indebted to Gilbert **Ryle** and Isaiah **Berlin**, who have 'discussed', and made 'valuable suggestions' about, all the points in 'this treatise' (pp. 10–11).

A. J. Ayer, 11 Foubert's Place, London, July 1935

Chapter 1
The Elimination of Metaphysics (pp. 13–29)

The 'traditional' philosophical disputes are 'unwarranted', and can be ended by clearly establishing the 'purpose and method' of 'philosophical inquiry' (p. 13). First, we may criticize the 'metaphysical thesis' that philosophy provides 'knowledge' of a 'reality' that transcends the 'world of science and common sense' (p. 13). In fact, one can be a 'metaphysician' without believing in such a reality, as many metaphysical statements arise from 'logical errors', rather than the wish to exceed the 'limits of **experience**'; but we can attack those who do believe in one, by asking about the '**premises**' from which they **deduce** their '**propositions**' (p. 13). They must begin with the 'evidence' of the 'senses', and, as nothing '**super-empirical**' can be **inferred** 'legitimately' from 'empirical premises', how are they able to reach 'a transcendent reality' (pp. 13–14)? The metaphysician's response might be that a '**faculty of intellectual intuition**' gives him access to facts that cannot be known from 'sense-experience'; and the best way to attack this position is to criticize the 'nature' of his propositions, for, as no proposition, referring to a transcendent reality, can have **'literal significance'**, any such proposition must be **'nonsense'** (p. 14).

It may be said that **Kant** has proved this already, but it was on 'different grounds': he argued that 'human understanding' cannot, in 'fact', go outside the 'limits of possible experience', as 'our minds' cannot penetrate beyond the **'phenomenal world'** (pp. 14–15). But my position is that it is fruitless to try and go beyond 'possible sense-experience', not because of the human mind's 'actual constitution', but because of 'the rule' that determines language's 'literal significance': the metaphysician's sentences are not 'literally significant' (p. 15). What is the 'criterion', by which we can test whether 'a sentence expresses a genuine proposition about a matter of fact' (pp. 15–16)? It is that of 'verifiability': a sentence is only 'factually significant' if the person uttering it knows what 'observations' would lead him to regard it as either 'true' or 'false' (p. 16). If it is 'consistent' with 'any assumption' about the 'nature of his future experience', then, though 'emotionally significant' for him, it is a 'pseudo-proposition', which is not literally significant, whatever its 'grammatical appearance' may suggest (p. 16).

We must distinguish between **'practical verifiability'** and **'verifiability in principle'** (p. 16). There are 'significant propositions' about 'matters of fact', such as there being 'mountains' on the far 'side of the moon', which we have no 'practical means' of verifying; but we know, in theory, what 'observations' would decide such a matter, so they are 'verifiable in principle' (p. 17). In contrast, a **metaphysical pseudo-proposition**, like **'the Absolute enters into, but is itself incapable of, evolution**

27

and progress', is unverifiable, 'even in principle': no conceivable observation could determine its truth or falsity (p. 17). And as 'the **author' of this remark** would have accepted that it was not meant to be either tautological, or capable of 'being verified' in principle, it lacks 'literal significance', even for him (pp. 17–18).

There is an important distinction between the **'strong' and 'weak' senses of verifiability** (p. 18). The first applies when the truth of a proposition can be 'conclusively established in experience', the second if there is the possibility of experience making it 'probable' (p. 18). As 'general propositions', like 'all men are mortal', cannot be 'established with certainty by any finite series of observations', making 'conclusive verifiability' the 'criterion of significance' would mean treating them like metaphysical 'statements' (p. 18). One **positivist** response has been to accept that 'general propositions' are an 'important type of nonsense', but this is unsatisfactory, as the problem also arises with 'propositions about the remote past', for no 'historical' statement can ever be more than 'highly probable' (pp. 18–19). Applying the 'principle' that only 'conclusively verifiable' sentences can be 'factually significant' would result in the impossibility of making any 'significant' factual statements (p. 19). Confining 'factually significant' sentences to those that are **'confutable by experience'** would be equally unacceptable (p. 19). It is no more possible to confute a **'hypothesis'** conclusively than to verify it conclusively (p. 19). We may think that a certain number of 'observations' would prove it false, but there is nothing self-contradictory in holding that 'some of the relevant circumstances' are different, and that it has not 'really broken down' (pp. 19–20).

We are forced back on the 'weaker sense of verification': of any **'putative statement of fact'**, we must ask whether 'any observations' are 'relevant' to determining its 'truth or false-hood' (p. 20). Only a 'negative answer' to this question would make it 'nonsensical' (p. 20). Thus, the 'mark' of a 'genuine factual proposition' is not that it should be 'equivalent to an **experiential proposition**' (one that records an 'actual or possible observation'), but that 'some experiential propositions' can be 'deduced from it', together with 'certain other premises', which could not be deduced from the 'other premises alone' (p. 20). What sort of assertions would this 'criterion' rule out as 'nonsensical' (p. 21)? One example is that 'the world of sense-experience' is 'unreal' (p. 21). True, 'our senses' deceive us at times, but 'further sense-experience' makes us aware of 'the mistakes': we depend on our senses to 'substantiate or confute' judgements, based on 'our **sensations**' (p. 21). Clearly, 'no conceivable observation' could show that the world, revealed to us by 'sense-experience', is 'unreal', so any statement that it is 'mere appearance, as opposed to reality', is 'literally nonsensical' (p. 21).

This 'criterion' forces us to 'condemn as fictitious' such controversies as that about how many '**substances**' there are 'in the world' (p. 21). No 'possible observation' is relevant to solving 'the dispute' between '**monists**', who say reality is 'one substance', and '**pluralists**', who say it is 'many', so 'neither assertion is significant' (pp. 21–2). The same is true of that 'between **realists** and **idealists**' (p. 22). Let us imagine that a picture is found, and attributed to **Goya**. Established procedures exist for determining the artist's identity. When these have been carried out, there may still be dissent, but everyone knows, and agrees about, the relevant 'empirical evidence' for deciding the matter (p. 22). But, what if some of those involved say that the picture is a 'set of ideas' in 'God's mind', and others that it is 'objectively real' (p. 22)? How could this dispute be settled? What 'process' exists for determining whether the picture is 'real', in the sense of being 'opposed to "ideal"' (p. 23)? By our criterion, the dispute between 'idealists and realists' is 'fictitious' (p. 23).

Thus, we must distinguish philosophy, as a 'genuine branch of knowledge', from metaphysics (p. 23). Some think that, historically, a lot of philosophy has been 'metaphysical', but most 'great philosophers' were not metaphysicians (p. 23). Further, I will establish below that 'all propositions' with 'factual content' are 'empirical hypotheses', the 'function' of which is to give a rule for anticipating experience (p. 23). They must be 'relevant to some actual, or possible, experience', or they are not empirical hypotheses, and so lack 'factual content': which is what 'the principle of verifiability asserts' (pp. 23–4). Of course, the 'nonsensical' nature of metaphysical 'utterances' does not follow from their lack of 'factual content' alone, but from this, together with their not being '*a priori* propositions' (the 'certainty' of which is due to their being 'tautologies') either (p. 24). Thus, a 'metaphysical sentence' is one that does not express either a 'tautology' or an 'empirical hypothesis'; and, as all 'significant propositions' belong to one or other of these two classes, 'all metaphysical assertions' must be 'nonsensical' (p. 24).

The term 'substance' illustrates how a lot of metaphysics 'comes to be written' (p. 24). We cannot refer to a thing's '**sensible properties**' without using language that seems to 'stand for the thing itself', as distinct from what is 'said about it' (p. 24). This leads those who believe that there must be a 'single real entity', corresponding to 'every name', to hold that we must 'distinguish logically' between 'the thing itself' and its 'sensible properties'; and they use 'the term "substance"' to refer to the former (p. 24). In referring to a thing's 'appearances', we do seem to distinguish it from them, but this is a mere 'accident of linguistic usage' (p. 25). 'Logical **analysis**' shows that what makes them '"appearances of" the same thing' is their 'relationship' to each other, not to 'an entity other than themselves' (p. 25).

Grammatical considerations may also account for our desire to 'raise questions about **Being**' (p. 25). Sentences expressing 'existential' and **'attributive' propositions** may have the 'same grammatical form', so they may be assumed to be of 'the same logical type': that, for example, the proposition, 'Martyrs exist', credits this group with an 'attribute', just as the proposition, 'Martyrs suffer', does, because both have 'a noun followed by an **intransitive verb**' (p. 25). However, Kant has shown that 'existence is not an attribute' (pp. 25–6). When we say something has an attribute, we 'covertly assert' it exists, but, if existence were 'an attribute', 'positive **existential propositions**' would be tautological, and 'negative' ones 'self-contradictory', which they are not (p. 26). A 'similar mistake' arises from the 'superficial grammatical resemblance' between 'unicorns are fictitious' and 'dogs are faithful' (p. 26). It is argued that to be fictitious unicorns must exist, but as it is 'self-contradictory' to maintain that 'fictitious objects' exist, they exist in 'some non-empirical sense' (p. 26). But this 'assertion' lacks 'literal significance': there is no way of 'testing' it, and it is made because it is assumed that 'being fictitious is an attribute' (p. 26). It is the view that there must be a 'real entity', corresponding to any 'word or phrase' that can be the 'subject of a sentence', which leads **Heidegger** to maintain that '**Nothing**' denotes 'something peculiarly mysterious' (pp. 26–7).

All this shows how 'easy' it is to write 'literally nonsensical' sentences, and that many 'traditional' philosophical problems are 'metaphysical' and 'fictitious' (p. 27). Sometimes, metaphysicians are regarded as being like poets, whose role is to 'express, or arouse, emotion' (p. 27). In fact, most of what poets write has 'literal meaning'; and, when they do write 'nonsense', it is because they consider it the most appropriate means of achieving their desired effect (p. 28). But the metaphysician 'does not intend to write nonsense'; he is deceived into it by 'grammar' or 'errors of reasoning' (p. 28). Of course, there are 'metaphysical passages' that express 'genuine **mystical** feeling', and they can be regarded as having 'moral or aesthetic value' (p. 29). But we must realize that 'the utterances', even of the metaphysician who is trying to 'expound a **vision**', are 'literally senseless', so that we may pursue philosophy with as little concern for them as for any other 'kind of metaphysics' (p. 29).

Chapter 2
The Function of Philosophy (pp. 30–47)

Abandoning metaphysics frees philosophy from 'the view' that it must 'construct a **deductive system**' of '**first principles**', which, with their 'consequences', will give a 'complete picture of reality' (p. 30). In fact, there are no 'first principles' that can function as a 'certain basis' of knowledge (p. 30). They are not to be 'found among' the '**laws of nature**', as these are just 'hypotheses', which 'experience' can confute (p. 30). But philosophical 'system-builders' have anyway preferred to base their systems on 'principles' they consider '**logically certain**', rather than '**inductive**' ones (p. 30). Thus, **Descartes** tried to base 'all human knowledge' on 'propositions' that it would be 'self-contradictory to deny', and thought that his *'cogito'*, which we should interpret as 'there is a thought now', was one (pp. 30–1). However, not only does *'non cogito'* not negate itself (no 'significant proposition' can), but his 'initial principle', '***cogito ergo sum***', is 'false': it does not follow from there being a thought that 'I exist' (p. 31). The occurrence of a thought, at a particular time, does not 'entail' the occurrence of another, or of 'a series' of them that is enough to 'constitute a single **self**' (p. 31). Hume showed that no 'one event **intrinsically** points' to another, so trying to base a 'deductive system' on propositions that describe the 'immediately given' inevitably fails (p. 31).

What about taking a 'set of *a priori* truths' as our 'first principles' (p. 31)? As already stated, such truths are 'tautologies', from which only 'further' ones can be 'validly deduced', and it would be 'absurd' to maintain that a 'set of tautologies' constituted the 'whole truth about the universe' (p. 31). Believing that the philosopher's role is to locate 'first principles' is connected to the view that philosophy's concern is to study 'reality as a whole'; and this, if it means that the philosopher can stand 'outside the world', to gain an overview of it, is a 'metaphysical conception' (p. 32). But, if it means that the philosopher's concern is with 'the content' of 'each of the sciences', it does express a partial 'truth' (p. 32). What we must resist is the 'delusion' that philosophy is a 'special department of **speculative knowledge**', which can give access to otherwise unattainable 'objects' of knowledge: 'in principle', no form of 'speculative knowledge' is outside the range of 'empirical science' (p. 32).

So, what is the nature of philosophy's 'critical activity' (p. 33)? It is not to 'test the validity' of 'scientific hypotheses' or 'everyday assumptions' (p. 33). Philosophy can draw attention to the 'criteria' for determining whether propositions are true or false, which may lead a '**sceptic**', who is questioning the truth of generally accepted propositions, to recognize that his 'original beliefs' are 'justified' (p. 33). But philosophy does not itself justify these beliefs; it simply points out that 'experience' does (p. 33). 'Empirical verification' is the only 'necessary or possible' justification for 'empirical propositions', and this is the case with both scientific hypotheses and the **'maxims of common sense'** (p. 33). The only difference between the two is that the former are 'more abstract', 'precise' and 'fruitful' (p. 34).

So, we must stop insisting that science lacks logical respectability until philosophers have 'solved the **problem of induction**', that is, identified a means of proving that 'empirical generalizations', drawn from 'past experience', will continue to apply 'in the future' (p. 34). Neither of the 'two ways' of tackling this so-called problem can solve it (p. 34). If we try to 'deduce' the proposition that needs to be proved from a 'purely formal principle', we make the mistake of thinking that a proposition about a 'matter of fact' can be deduced from 'a tautology' (p. 34). But, if we try to deduce it from an 'empirical principle', we assume what we are attempting to prove: we cannot, 'for example', base our justification for **'induction'** on the **'uniformity of nature'**, as this principle assumes the reliability of 'past experience' as a 'guide to the future' (p. 34).

The 'problem of induction' cannot be solved, because it is 'fictitious': apart from 'self-consistency', the only relevant test of a 'scientific procedure' is that it works, so enabling us to 'predict future experience' and to 'control our environment' (p. 35). There is no 'logical guarantee' that this will go on being the case, but it is an error to ask for one, as it is 'logically impossible to obtain' (p. 35). Regrettably, philosophers, interested in the 'so-called **theory of knowledge**', overlook this point (p. 35). They think that we are not justified in believing that 'material things' exist, without a satisfactory analysis of 'perception' (pp. 35–6). But what entitles us to believe in them is having 'certain sensations': the sole basis of the 'validity' of 'perceptual judgements' is 'actual sense-experience' (p. 36). Again, philosophers should not be contemptuous of 'common sense' beliefs, only critical of 'unreflecting analysis' of them, which treats 'grammatical structure' as a sure 'guide' to 'meaning' (p. 36). For example, many of the problems relating to perception are associated with the **metaphysical notion of "substance"**, and arise from the impossibility of referring to something without seeming to 'distinguish it generically from its qualities and states' (p. 36). The philosopher's task is not searching for 'speculative truths' or 'first principles', but 'clarification and analysis' (pp. 36–7).

This does not mean that everyone regarded as a philosopher has been concerned with analysis: much so-called philosophy has been 'metaphysical' (p. 37). The purpose of our enquiry into philosophy's 'function' is to find a definition, which is consistent with 'the practice' of those who are generally regarded as philosophers and also with the view that philosophy is a 'special branch of knowledge' (p. 37). Metaphysics, though widely held to be part of philosophy, does not meet the 'second condition', and so must be distinguished from it (p. 37). Some will think that this conclusion will confuse those who have been 'taught' to regard metaphysics as philosophy (p. 37). However, the 'history of philosophy' is not just that of metaphysics, and most 'great philosophers' were not 'metaphysicians', but 'analysts' (p. 38). For example, **Locke**'s *Essay Concerning Human Understanding* is 'analytic', and, like Moore's today, his is a philosophy of 'common sense', which (again like Moore's) does not attempt '*a priori* justification' of 'common sense beliefs', but only analysis of them (p. 38). Locke defines 'knowledge', classifies 'propositions', and shows the 'nature of material things' (p. 38). Berkeley is not 'a metaphysician' either, as he denied not the 'reality' of 'material things' but the 'adequacy' of Locke's 'analysis' of the 'notion' of them (pp. 38–9). Rightly, he held that regarding certain 'ideas of sensation' as belonging to a 'single material thing' does not mean, as Locke maintained, that they belong to a 'single unobservable underlying "somewhat"', but that they stand in 'relations' to each other (p. 39). He realized that material things must be defined 'in terms of **sense-contents**', but he was misled by the word '**idea**', to 'denote' what is 'given in sensation', into thinking that it is 'necessarily mental'; and this resulted in some 'paradoxical conclusions', including postulating 'God' as the 'unobservable cause of our "ideas"' (pp. 39–40). Clearly, as Berkeley realized, material things must be defined 'in terms of sense-contents', because it is only through the latter's 'occurrence' that we can verify the former's 'existence' (p. 39). So, the question we have to answer is not whether a 'phenomenalist "theory of perception"' is true, but only 'what form' it takes (p. 39).

Hume 'explicitly rejected metaphysics', as the closing words (about committing **books of 'divinity'** and '**school metaphysics**' to 'the flames') of the *Enquiry Concerning Human Understanding* indicate (p. 40). This is a 'rhetorical version' of our view that sentences which are not 'formally true' propositions, or 'empirical' hypotheses, lack 'literal significance' (p. 40). His 'works' are analytical, although this is sometimes challenged, due to his 'treatment of **causation**' (which he sought to define) being 'misinterpreted' as denial of it (p. 40). Hume saw that the truth or falsity of 'causal' propositions cannot be 'settled *a priori*', and his analysis of causation shows that: the 'relation of cause and effect' is not 'logical in character', as denying propositions that state a 'causal connexion' is not self-contradictory; 'causal laws' are not 'analytically derived from experience', because they cannot be deduced from a 'finite number of experiential propositions'; and it is erroneous to 'analyse' propositions which state 'causal connexions' in terms of necessary relations between 'particular events', as there are no conceivable 'observations' on which such relations can be based (pp. 40–1). And, while we reject Hume's 'actual definitions of a cause', we essentially agree with him about the 'nature of causation' (p. 42). Asserting a 'particular causal connexion' involves asserting a 'causal law', and general propositions of the type, 'C causes E', are 'equivalent' to propositions of the type, 'whenever C, then E', with the 'whenever' referring, not to a 'finite number of actual instances of C', but to the 'infinite number' of 'possible' ones (p. 41). He is also right that 'success in practice' is the only 'justification for inductive reasoning'; and, had he made this point clearly, might have avoided the 'air of paradox' that attaches to his work, and causes it to be 'undervalued and misunderstood' (p. 42).

Hobbes and **Bentham** were mainly concerned with 'giving definitions', while **Mill**'s 'best' work was developing Hume's 'analyses': indeed, that 'philosophizing is essentially analytic' is 'implicit in **English empiricism**' (p. 42). **Plato**, **Aristotle** and Kant are also 'great philosophers' who have been 'predominantly' concerned with analysis (p. 42). But, even if no philosophers matched our 'definition of philosophy', it would not make it wrong, given 'our initial **postulates**': the distinction we have made between 'our sense' of philosophy and metaphysics is a valid one (p. 43).

Philosophy is 'independent' of metaphysics, and 'philosophical analysis' does not have a 'metaphysical basis' (p. 43). Analysis is not about dissecting objects into their 'constituent parts', in order to exhibit the universe as an '**aggregate of "bare particulars"**' (anyway, 'no possible observation' could verify such 'an assertion') (p. 43). The 'analytic method' would be 'faulty', if it involved denying that the world contains many 'complex objects', which are more than the 'sum of their parts' (pp. 43–4). These are '**genuine wholes**', not 'mere aggregates', and, if an '**atomistic metaphysics**' led the 'analyst' to hold that an object, comprising 'parts *a*, *b*, *c* and *d*', in a 'distinctive' combination, was no more than '*a* + *b* + *c* + *d*', he would give a 'false account of its nature' (pp. 43–4). But the analytic method does not depend on any 'metaphysical', or even 'empirical', 'presupposition' about the 'nature of things': its concern is not with an object's 'physical properties', but with how 'we speak about them' (p. 44). Philosophical propositions are 'linguistic', not 'factual', expressing 'definitions', or their 'formal consequences' (p. 44). Philosophy is a 'department of logic', and, as its propositions differ 'in type' from 'scientific' ones, science and philosophy cannot 'contradict' each other (p. 44). Further, the latter's role of providing 'definitions' plainly does not involve any 'nonsensical' assertions about the world consisting of 'bare particulars', or any such 'metaphysical **dogma**' (pp. 44–5).

The problem is that the way they are expressed can make 'linguistic' propositions look like 'factual' ones (p. 45). For example, the statement that a 'material thing cannot be in two places at once' looks like an 'empirical' proposition, and there are those who think this shows the logical certainty of some 'empirical' propositions (p. 45). However, it relates to our 'use' of 'the relevant words', and so is a 'linguistic' proposition that does not, in any way, indicate 'certain knowledge' of the 'empirical properties of objects' (p. 45). Again, the proposition, '**Relations are not particulars, but universals**', seems to state an 'empirical' fact, but concerns 'words', not 'things': that, 'by definition', '**relation-symbols**' belong to the 'class of **symbols** for characters', not 'things' (pp. 45–6). Philosophy asks many apparently 'factual' questions, of the type, 'What is an *x*', or its 'nature'?, but these are 'requests for definitions' (p. 46). We must not be 'deceived' by this use of '"factual" language' into thinking that philosophy is an 'empirical' or 'metaphysical inquiry': when the philosopher refers to analysis of 'facts, or notions', he refers to 'the definition of the corresponding words' (pp. 46–7).

Chapter 3
The Nature of Philosophical Analysis (pp. 48–63)

Philosophy's being about 'definitions' does not mean that its function is 'to compile a dictionary': its concern is not with '*explicit* definitions', but with '**definitions** *in use*' (p. 48). The former is providing 'another symbol' that is '**synonymous**' with the first; two symbols are synonymous if substituting one for the other, in a sentence, always produces a new sentence that is 'equivalent to the old' (p. 48). In 'ordinary discourse', most definitions are '*explicit*', as with 'oculist' being defined as 'eye-doctor' (p. 49). A '**symbol** *in use*' is defined not by saying it is synonymous 'with some other symbol', but by showing how sentences, in which 'it significantly occurs', can be 'translated into equivalent sentences', containing neither the '*definiendum*', nor 'any of its synonyms' (p. 49). **Russell's 'theory of definite descriptions'** states that all sentences containing this form of 'symbolic expression' can be 'translated' into ones which do not 'contain any such expression', but do have a 'sub-sentence asserting that one, and only one, object possesses a certain property', or that 'no one object possesses' it (pp. 49–50). Thus, 'The round square cannot exist' is 'equivalent to "No one thing can be both square and round"', while, 'The **author of *Waverley*** was Scotch' becomes 'One person, and one person only, wrote *Waverley*, and that person was Scotch'

(p. 50). The first shows how to eliminate 'any definite descriptive phrase', occurring as 'the subject of a negative existential sentence', while the second illustrates how to do so with 'any definite descriptive phrase', occurring 'anywhere in any other type of sentence' (p. 50). They show us how to express 'what is expressed by any sentence' containing a 'definite descriptive phrase', without using such a phrase, and so give us 'a definition of these phrases in use' (p. 50).

This 'definition of descriptive phrases' enables us to understand 'certain sentences' better (p. 50). Those who believe that there are such 'subsistent entities' as a 'round square' indicate, by their 'lapse into metaphysics', a 'naïve assumption that definite descriptive phrases are **demonstrative symbols**': Russell's definition, by revealing the 'logical complexity' of certain sentences, shows this assumption to be 'false' (pp. 50–1). The role of 'philosophical' definitions is to 'dispel' the 'confusions' arising from inadequate understanding of 'certain types of sentence', where this cannot be done by substituting a 'synonym for any symbol', either because none exists, or because the synonym is 'unclear' for the same reasons that the symbol is (p. 51).

A complete 'system of definitions in use' would reveal a language's 'structure' (p. 51). One complicating 'factor' is that many symbols, such as 'is', are '**ambiguous**', consisting of 'signs' that are 'identical in their **sensible form**' with 'one another', or with signs from another 'symbol': what makes two signs 'elements of the same symbol' is not only 'identity of form', but also 'of usage' (p. 52). We might assume that the 'is' in 'He is the author of that book', is the same as that in 'A cat is a mammal'; but the first sentence is equivalent to, 'He, and no one else, wrote that book', the second to, 'The class of mammals contains the class of cats' (p. 52).

Chapter 3: The Nature of Philosophical Analysis

Saying a symbol is 'constituted by signs' that are 'identical' in their 'sensible form' and 'significance', and that a sign is a 'sense-content', used to 'convey literal meaning', is not to say that a symbol is a 'collection' of sense-contents (p. 52). To refer to 'certain objects' ('*b, c, d*') as 'elements' of another ('*e*'), is not to say that they are 'part' of it, in the way an 'arm' is of a 'body', but that sentences in which 'the symbol *e* occurs' can be 'translated' into ones in which it does not, but '*b, c, d*' do (pp. 52–3). It is a '**logical construction**' from them; and the 'symbols', denoting 'logical constructions', make it possible to 'state complicated propositions' about the latter 'in a relatively simple form' (p. 53). Logical constructions are not 'fictitious objects' (p. 53). The 'notion of a logical construction' is a 'linguistic assertion', indicating that a particular symbol can be defined 'in terms of certain symbols' that stand for 'sense-contents, not explicitly, but in use' (p. 53). So, a sentence containing 'the symbol "table"' can be translated into one in which that symbol does not occur, but in which 'certain symbols', standing for sense-contents, do (pp. 53–4).

The 'problem' of devising a rule for 'translating sentences' about material things into ones about 'sense-contents' (the '**reduction**' of the former to the latter) is the principal 'philosophical' element of the '**problem of perception**' (p. 54). Those who write about perception, and try to describe the 'nature' of material things, think they are addressing a 'factual question'; but it is a 'linguistic' one, 'being a demand for a definition' (pp. 54–5). The propositions required to answer it concern the 'relationship of symbols', not the 'properties' of the things 'the symbols' denote (p. 55). But, as we are unable to 'describe the properties of sense-contents' precisely, it is 'convenient' to express the 'solution' of the problem of perception in 'factual terminology' (p. 55). We talk of constructing 'material

41

things out of sense-contents', and indicate their 'relationship' by 'showing' the 'principles of this "construction"': we answer questions about a material thing's nature by indicating 'the relations' that need to obtain between 'any two' of our sense-contents for them to be 'elements of the same material thing' (p. 55).

Our 'solution' of the problem of perception illustrates the 'method of philosophical analysis' (p. 55). Two 'sense-contents' can be said to 'resemble' each other 'directly' when they differ only minutely in 'quality'; 'indirectly', when they are connected by a 'series of direct resemblances', but are not 'directly **resemblant**' (pp. 55–6). Two 'visual, or **tactual**, sense-contents' are 'directly continuous' when they 'belong to successive members of a series of actual, or possible **sense-fields**', and, at most, differ only minutely with regard to 'the position' of each in its own 'sense-field'; and indirectly, when 'an actual, or possible, series of such direct continuities' relates them (p. 56). To say that sense-experiences, fields or contents are 'possible', rather than 'actual', is not to say that they have occurred (or will), but would under specifiable 'conditions' (p. 56). Thus, we may say that any two of our 'visual' or 'tactual sense-contents' are 'elements' of the same 'material' object, if linked by relations of certain kinds of 'direct, or indirect, resemblance' and 'continuity' (p. 56). Further, the 'groups of visual and tactual sense-contents', 'constituted by means of these relations', cannot have 'members in common': no 'sense-content can be an element of more than one material thing' (p. 57).

How are these 'visual and tactual' sense-contents 'correlated' (p. 57)? Any two 'belong to the same material thing', when 'every element of the visual group' that is of 'minimal visual depth', is part of the 'same sense-experience' as one from the 'tactual group' that is of 'minimal tactual depth'

42

(p. 57). 'Depth' can only be **defined 'ostensively'**, but one sense-content has more 'depth than another', when further from 'the observer's body' (p. 57). With sense-contents of 'taste, or sound, or smell' 'assigned to particular material things', they are 'classified' by referring to their 'association with tactual sense-contents' (p. 58). For example, we 'assign' taste sense-contents to the same 'material things' as those to which we assign the sense-contents of 'touch' that the 'tongue' is experiencing at the same time (p. 58).

What about 'a rule' for translating 'sentences', referring to material things' '"real" qualities' (p. 58)? A 'certain quality' is a particular material thing's 'real quality', if it 'characterizes' the 'elements' of the thing that are 'most conveniently measured' (p. 58). For example, a coin's being 'really round in shape' does not mean that the 'sense-content' is, or that all its 'visual, or tactual, elements' are, but that 'roundness' 'characterizes' the 'elements of the coin' that are 'experienced' from the standpoint from which 'measurements of shape' are 'most conveniently' made (p. 58). This 'outline' of a definition of 'symbols' that 'stand for material things' is designed to help us understand the sentences, in which we 'refer' to the latter, better (p. 59). People understand a 'simple' statement like, 'This is a table', but may be unaware of its 'logical complexity', and thus inclined to accept some 'metaphysical belief' about the 'existence of material substances' (p. 59). The 'philosophical' definition's value is to dispel these 'confusions' (p. 59).

We have avoided the 'highly ambiguous' term, 'meaning', and referred instead to sentences having 'the **relation of equivalence**' (p. 60). Saying two sentences have 'the same meaning' often signifies that they affect people's 'thoughts' in the same way (p. 60). However, two sentences can be 'equivalent', by 'our criterion', but produce 'very different psychological' effects (p. 60). For example, '*p* is a law of nature', is 'equivalent to', '*p* is a general hypothesis which can always be relied on' (60). But, in this context, the word 'law' has connotations of 'orderliness' in nature that are not 'evoked by the equivalent sentence' (p. 60). Again, it is 'misleading' to say that 'philosophy' shows the actual use of 'certain symbols' (p. 61). 'The author of *Waverley* was Scotch', is 'equivalent to', 'One person, and one person only, wrote *Waverley*, and that person was Scotch', but this is not to assert that those who speak English 'use these sentences interchangeably', only that every sentence 'entailed' by the first and 'any given group of sentences', is also entailed by the second (p. 61). 'Philosophical analysis' is a 'purely logical activity'; it is not concerned with 'empirical study' of a particular group's 'linguistic habits' (p. 62). When 'the philosopher' specifies the language to which 'his definitions' apply, he just describes the '**conventions**' from which they are 'deduced' (p. 62). Generally, these correspond to those used, but such 'correspondence' is not 'part of what the definitions actually assert' (p. 62). An '**artificial system of symbols**', like that in Russell and **Whitehead's** *Principia Mathematica*, assists analysis of 'a language', but Carnap has shown that a language can be used in 'analysis of itself' (pp. 62–3).

Chapter 4
The *A Priori* (pp. 64–83)

'Analysis' is 'implicit' in the 'practice' of 'traditional' **empiricists**, and our view is that philosophy is a 'form of empiricism' (p. 64). But this raises the common 'objection' to all types of empiricism: they cannot explain 'knowledge of **necessary truths**' (p. 64). However frequently a general proposition is 'verified' in 'experience', it can never be 'logically certain', as

Chapter 4: The A Priori

it could be 'confuted' in the 'future' (p. 64). No proposition concerning a 'matter of fact' can be demonstrated to be 'necessarily and universally true' (pp. 64–5). But it does not follow that we are 'irrational' to 'believe it': what is 'irrational' is to insist on 'certainty', for, with all scientific and common sense '"truths"', only 'probability' is obtainable (p. 65).

However, there is a problem with '**formal logic** and mathematics', as their 'truths' seem 'necessary and certain' (p. 65). So, the 'empiricist' must either deny that they are, or accept that they lack 'factual content' (p. 65). If neither course is 'satisfactory', we shall have to accept '**rationalism**', and admit that there are 'truths' that can be known 'independently of experience' (p. 66). But doing so would overturn this book's 'main argument', which is that sentences say 'nothing', unless 'empirically verifiable' (p. 66). On the other hand, if one of the alternatives stated above can be shown to be 'correct', rationalism's 'foundations' will be 'destroyed', as it claims that 'thought' is an 'independent source of knowledge', which is more reliable than experience (p. 66). We shall have established the 'empiricist contention' that there are no 'truths of reason' that 'refer to matters of fact' (p. 67).

Mill espoused the first alternative, arguing that logical and mathematical 'truths' are not 'necessary or certain', but 'inductive generalizations', based on very many 'supporting instances', which differ from scientific 'hypotheses' not 'in kind' but in their degree of probability (p. 67). He considered them to be highly successful, but 'theoretically fallible', 'empirical hypotheses' (p. 67). But Mill's claim that logical and mathematical propositions have the 'same status as empirical hypotheses' is unacceptable (p. 68). Saying we know them 'independently of experience' means their 'validity' is not decided by 'empirical verification' (pp. 67–8). But, however we learn about them, once 'apprehended' they are seen, unlike 'empirical generalizations', to be 'necessarily' true (p. 68). Thus, Mill's theory is at odds with the 'relevant logical facts' and incorrect (p. 68).

To confirm our view that logical and mathematical 'truths' are 'necessarily' true, we will consider cases where such a truth appears to be (but is not) 'confuted' (pp. 68–9). If I count what I take to be 'five pairs of objects', but there are only nine, I do not think that the 'mathematical proposition "$2 \times 5 = 10$"' has been proved wrong, but that I have miscounted (p. 69). Again, we do not conclude that the 'mathematical proposition' that the angles of a '**Euclidean triangle**' add up to '180 degrees' is wrong, if the angles of what looks like one do not amount to this total (p. 69). We take it that our measurements were wrong, or that the triangle is not 'Euclidean' (p. 69). Whenever mathematical truths seem to be in doubt, we 'preserve' their 'validity' by finding another 'explanation' (p. 69). It is the same with the 'principles of formal logic', such as the '**law of excluded middle**': that it is 'impossible' that neither a proposition, nor its 'contradictory', should be 'true' (p. 70). We 'preserve' this logical principle by indicating that 'negating' a sentence does not always produce 'the contradictory' of the original proposition (p. 70).

Mill was 'wrong' to think that logical or mathematical truths can be overthrown (p. 71). They are 'universally' true, because we ensure that they are: we cannot discard them without 'contradicting ourselves', and breaching linguistic 'rules' (p. 71). Both kinds of truth are 'analytic propositions or tautologies' (p. 71). Kant defines an 'analytic proposition' as one in which 'the predicate B' is included in 'the concept' of the 'subject A', such that the predicate adds 'nothing' to the subject, whereas a '**synthetic**' proposition adds to 'the subject' a predicate, not in any way 'thought in it' (p. 71). Thus, 'all bodies are extended' is 'analytic', whereas 'all bodies are heavy' is 'synthetic' (p. 71). But, he also considers '7 + 5 = 12' to be 'synthetic', because 'twelve' is not 'already thought' in 'thinking' of the combination of 'seven and five' (pp. 71–2).

Kant's 'distinction' between the two kinds of proposition lacks clarity, because he offers more than one criterion (p. 72). He regards '7 + 5' as 'synthetic', because the **subjective intension**' of it does not 'comprise' that of '12', but his view that 'all bodies are extended' is 'analytic' is based solely on the 'principle of contradiction' (p. 72). Thus, he gives both a 'psychological' and a 'logical criterion'; and, most pertinently, just because it is possible to think of '7 + 5' without 'necessarily thinking' of 12, it does not follow that it is not self-contradictory to deny that it is the sum of the first two numbers (pp. 72–3). We can eliminate the 'confusions' of Kant's account by saying that the 'validity' of an analytic proposition is wholly dependent on 'the definitions of the symbols it contains', while that of a synthetic one is decided by 'experience' (p. 73). Analytic propositions do not give 'information' about matters of fact, and so cannot be confuted by 'experience' (p. 73). But, unlike 'metaphysical utterances', they are not 'senseless', for they clarify our 'use' of 'certain symbols' (p. 74). For example, 'if all Bretons are Frenchmen, and all Frenchmen Europeans, then all Bretons are Europeans', gives no factual information, but does illustrate the 'convention' governing the use of 'if' and 'all' (p. 74).

An 'encyclopaedia' of all our factual 'information' would not include any 'analytic propositions', but we would use them to ensure that all our 'synthetic' ones were 'self-consistent' and free of 'contradictions' (p. 75). In **'traditional logic'**, **'formal' truths** were 'insufficiently formalized', and seemed to be about how 'thought' works, not (as they should be) with 'the **formal relationship of classes**' (p. 75). Russell and Whitehead's '**propositional calculus**' makes it plain that 'formal logic' is not to do with the 'properties' of 'minds' or 'objects', but with 'the possibility' of using 'logical particles' to combine 'propositions' into 'analytic' ones, and with their 'formal relationship', whereby one can be deduced from another (p. 76). Unlike '**Aristotelian logic**', in their 'system' every 'logical truth' serves as a '**principle of inference**', and Aristotle's '**laws of thought**' (those of '**identity**', 'excluded middle' and '**non-contradiction**') are not regarded as having greater importance than other 'analytic propositions' (p. 76). Further (a point that Russell did not perhaps appreciate), 'logical' propositions are 'valid' in their 'own right', and not just as part of 'a system': a '**symbolism**' can be conceived in which it can be seen that 'every analytic proposition' is 'analytic' through 'its form alone' (pp. 76–7).

Thus, even if mathematical propositions are not 'reducible to propositions of formal logic', they, too, are 'analytic' propositions, the 'criterion' of which is that their 'validity' follows from 'the definition' of the terms they contain (p. 77). One might think, along with Kant, that the 'propositions of geometry' are 'synthetic', as they seem to concern the 'properties of physical space' (p. 77). But the development of '**non-Euclidean geometries**' shows that geometrical '**axioms**' are just 'definitions' with '**theorems**' setting out their 'logical consequences' (p. 78). Thus, a particular geometry is not 'about physical space', but geometry can be applied to it (p. 78). The fact that many of us need diagrams in order to understand the implications of geometrical 'axioms' does not show that the 'relation' between the two is not a 'logical' one, but that our 'intellects' are limited (p. 79). Thus, we can reject Kant's view that mathematical propositions are 'synthetic': they are 'analytic propositions', or 'tautologies' (pp. 79–80).

Analytic propositions merely show 'our determination to use words' in a particular way (p. 80). Wittgenstein is right: our 'justification' for maintaining the inconceivability of the 'world' disobeying the 'laws of logic' is our inability to say what such a world would be like (p. 80). And, just as an 'analytic' proposition's 'validity' is 'independent of the nature of the external world', so also it is 'of the nature of our minds': whatever our 'linguistic conventions', analytic propositions would always be necessary (pp. 80–1). There is no mystery about the **'apodeictic certainty'** of logical and mathematical propositions: '7 + 5' will always be '12', and an 'oculist' an 'eye-doctor', because these 'symbolic' expressions are 'synonymous'; as **Poincaré** put it: mathematics is 'an immense tautology' (p. 81).

Yet, 'logic and mathematics' can be 'interesting' and 'surprising': why is this (p. 82)? Like their 'usefulness', it is due to the 'limitations of our reason' (p. 82). A being with an 'infinitely powerful' intellect would see all the implications of 'his definitions', but we have to use such forms of 'calculation' as the 'multiplication tables' in arithmetic and the 'laws of logic' (rules for transforming 'sentences expressed in logical symbolism' or 'ordinary language'), in order to work out their implications (pp. 82–3). Our tendency to make mistakes, and so 'contradict ourselves', when performing these processes, explains why there are 'logical and mathematical "falsehoods"' (p. 83). By inventing 'symbolic devices' for expressing 'highly complex tautologies' simply, we can minimize these (p. 83). Such 'well-chosen' definitions also make us aware of 'analytic truths' we may have overlooked (p. 83).

Only their being 'analytic' satisfactorily explains the '*a priori* necessity' of logical and mathematical 'truths' (p. 83). The empiricists are right: there is no '*a priori* knowledge of reality', and any truths known to be 'valid independently of all experience' are so through lack of 'factual content' (p. 83). They may 'guide' our 'search for knowledge', but tell us nothing about 'any matter of fact' (p. 83).

Chapter 5
Truth and Probability (pp. 84–103)

We shall now 'complete our theory of truth' by indicating how the 'validity of empirical propositions' is determined (p. 84). But first we should 'justify' the view that a 'theory of truth' only concerns the issue of 'how propositions are validated', and is not about answering a metaphysical question about the nature of truth (p. 84). In fact, when we ask, 'What is truth?' we are asking whether '(the proposition) *p* is true' (p. 85). It will be argued that we also say that 'statements', 'judgements', 'opinions' and so on are 'true or false', but these are just **elliptical** ways of referring to the truth or falsity of a proposition (p. 85). The 'is true' in '*p* is true' is 'logically superfluous': to say that '"Queen Anne is dead" is true' is just to say, 'Queen Anne is dead' (pp. 85–6). '"True" and "false" connote nothing': they simply signify 'assertion' or 'denial', so there is no 'sense' in trying to 'analyse the concept of "truth"' (p. 86). Why do so many philosophers think there is? The grammatical form of sentences containing the word 'true' suggests that it stands for a 'genuine quality or relation'; but, when the sentences are analysed, they are found to 'confirm our assumption' that 'What is truth?' is 'reducible' to 'What is the analysis of the sentence "*p* is true"?' (pp. 86–7). When the 'speculative' philosopher asks about the 'something real' that the 'word "truth"' appears to 'stand for', there is no satisfactory answer, because it is not a legitimate question (p. 87).

The question we need to answer is, 'What makes a proposition true or false': how are propositions 'validated' (p. 87)? The 'criterion' we use to decide the 'validity' of 'analytic' propositions is inadequate for determining that of 'empirical or synthetic' ones, which can be 'false', even if they are not 'self-contradictory' (p. 88). Some philosophers maintain that there is a 'special class' of **ostensive** 'empirical propositions', which are validated by their 'directly' recording 'an immediate experience', and which are 'absolutely certain' (p. 88). But we deny that a 'synthetic proposition' can be 'purely ostensive', as this is a 'contradiction in terms' (p. 89). It is logically impossible for there to be an 'intelligible' sentence, consisting solely of 'demonstrative symbols' (p. 89). Linguistically, we cannot indicate something but not describe it. A sentence expressing a proposition must say something about a 'situation', not just 'name' it, and this description not only registers a 'sense-content', but moves 'beyond' the 'immediately given', and classifies it (p. 89). Propositions relating to 'material things' are 'not ostensive': they refer to 'an infinite series of actual and possible sense-contents' (p. 90). For example, when we state that something 'is white', and this is taken as referring to 'a sense-content', not an object, we are stating that it is 'similar' to others we do, or have, 'called, white' (p. 90). Further, we might conclude that our 'classification' of the 'sense-content' was wrong; but this means that it is not an 'ostensive' proposition, as it would not be legitimate to doubt one that was (pp. 90–1). The 'only examples' of so-called 'ostensive propositions', which have been given, are those that describe 'the actual qualities of presented sense-contents'; and, if they are not 'ostensive', 'none are' (p. 91). The view that there are such propositions probably arises from the 'logical' error of identifying propositions which refer to our 'sensations' with the sensations themselves (p. 92). So, 'empirical propositions' are all 'hypotheses', the truth or falsity of which is determined by 'actual sense-experience' (p. 92). 'Logically', the process of verifying them could 'continue indefinitely': we may 'doubt' particular observations (pp. 92–3). However, for 'pragmatic' reasons, explained below, we generally regard 'certain types' as 'trustworthy' (p. 93).

Saying that 'hypotheses' are 'verified in experience' means not just one, but a 'system' (p. 93). When we test the 'validity' of a 'scientific "law"', by stating that, if 'certain conditions' obtain, a certain 'observation' will always be made, and we then make the observation, we also confirm the 'hypotheses' that assert the 'existence' of the 'conditions' (p. 93). If we do not make the 'expected observation', we are not compelled to accept that our 'law' is invalid: we may conclude that the 'conditions' were not as they seemed, or that some relevant 'factor' has been missed (p. 93). We can explain 'our observations' as we wish, but must avoid 'self-contradiction': we cannot maintain 'incompatible hypotheses' (p. 94). But, though we cling to 'cherished' hypotheses, against observations that seem to disprove them, the 'possibility' of our giving them up must exist, otherwise they are not 'genuine' hypotheses, but definitions, and so 'analytic', not 'synthetic' (p. 94).

It can be difficult to distinguish 'genuine hypotheses' from 'definitions', as with some 'laws of nature' (pp. 94–5). If 'experience' shows that all things of a certain type, 'A', have the 'property' of being 'B', we often make it a 'defining characteristic' of 'A', so that, 'All A's are B's' becomes a 'tautology', not a 'synthetic generalization' (p. 95). 'All men are mortal' is often cited as an example of a 'necessary' connection (p. 95).

But what is 'necessarily connected' here is the inclusion of 'the concept of "being mortal" in the 'concept of "man"', so that the 'word "man"' is used only of beings that are 'mortal', making 'All men are mortal' a tautology, not an empirical 'hypothesis' (pp. 95–6). Philosophers, who claim it is an example of 'necessary' connection, do not think it is 'a tautology', but are able to maintain that it is a 'synthetic and necessary' general proposition only because they 'tacitly' identify it with the 'tautology' (p. 96). Turning 'general propositions' into 'definitions' makes them 'necessary', but they then cease to be the 'original generalizations', which (as Hume pointed out) can 'never be necessary', as experience may invalidate them (p. 96).

What 'considerations' influence decisions about which hypotheses we should retain or discard (p. 96)? We do not ignore 'inconvenient observations', but make changes to our 'system', despite wishing to 'keep it intact' (p. 97). To answer this question, we need to recognize that the function of a system of 'hypotheses' is to 'enable us' to predict 'future experience' accurately, thus helping us 'to survive' (p. 97). 'Past experience' guides our 'predictions': we expect the 'future course of our sensations' to follow the same course as 'past' ones (pp. 98–9). We accept that if experience has shown that our 'system' has failed, it will probably do so again, and that ignoring the fact will not serve us as well as changing it, to make it a 'more efficient instrument' for anticipating 'experience' (pp. 98–9). Further, while we prefer minor adjustments to major alterations, if experience indicates the need for 'radical changes', we implement them, rather than face more 'disappointments'; and, if the 'new system' does not work, we change it again (p. 99). Thus, we 'test' an empirical proposition's 'validity' by checking whether it discharges its intended 'function' of anticipating 'experience' (pp. 99–100). If it does, its 'probability' is increased, although 'future' observations could still invalidate it (p. 100).

When we refer to observations increasing the 'probability' of a proposition, we are not talking about an 'intrinsic property' of it, but our greater degree of 'confidence' in it as a predictor of 'the future' (p. 100). To deal with 'all hypotheses' uniformly, we should always observe 'certain standards of evidence' when forming 'our beliefs', but we do not always do so, and so are not consistently 'rational' (p. 101). Our confidence in modern scientific 'methods' derives from their working 'in practice', but if we adopted 'different methods', 'in the future', we might come to regard current beliefs as 'irrational' (p. 101). Another way of saying that observations increase a hypothesis' 'probability' is to say that they add to the 'degree of confidence' that it is 'rational' to place in it, with a belief's 'rationality' being 'defined' not in relation to an 'absolute standard' but to 'part of our own actual practice' (pp. 101–2). At times, we may be wrong about the 'probability of a proposition', but our 'definition of probability' is 'compatible' with our being mistaken about the 'probability' of those we believe (p. 102). So, all 'synthetic' propositions are rules for anticipating 'future experience', and 'the fact' that those that refer to the 'past' have the 'same hypothetical character' as those that refer to the 'present' and 'future' does not mean that the 'three types' are not 'distinct', for they 'predict' different experiences (p. 102). 'Propositions about the past' are 'hypotheses', which give 'rules' for predicting '"historical" experiences' that can 'verify' them (pp. 102–3). Philosophers who disagree appear to make the erroneous assumption that 'the past' is 'objectively there', and 'real' in some 'metaphysical sense' (p. 103).

Chapter 6
Critique of Ethics and Theology (pp. 104–26)

We must meet a further 'objection', before we can justify our view that 'all synthetic propositions are empirical hypotheses' (p. 104). Some argue that 'speculative knowledge' is of two kinds, 'empirical fact' and **'questions of value'** (**'ethics** and **aesthetics'**), and that statements of the latter are 'genuine synthetic propositions' (p. 104). Therefore, we need to account satisfactorily for **'judgements of value'**, in a way that fits in with 'our general empiricist principles', by showing that they are either 'ordinary "scientific" statements', or 'expressions of emotion', which are neither 'true nor false' and not literally 'significant' (p. 104).

Ethical systems are not **'homogeneous'** (pp. 104–5). As well as elements of 'metaphysics' and **'analyses of non-ethical concepts'**, the 'ethical contents' themselves include **'definitions of ethical terms'** and 'judgements' about their 'legitimacy'; descriptions of the **'phenomena of moral experience, and their causes'**; **'exhortations to moral virtue'**; and 'actual ethical judgements' (p. 105). 'Ethical philosophers' tend not to distinguish these 'classes', but propositions about 'ethical terms' constitute the whole of 'ethical philosophy' (p. 105). The other classes belong to 'psychology, or sociology'; are 'commands', intended to get people to act in certain ways; or, as they are 'neither definitions' nor 'comments' about them, are not part of 'ethical philosophy' (p. 105). A 'strictly philosophical treatise on ethics' should not make 'ethical pronouncements', but analyse 'ethical terms' (p. 105).

Can 'statements of ethical value' be 'translated into statements of empirical fact' (p. 106)? **'Subjectivists'**, who define the 'rightness of actions, and the goodness of ends' in terms of the 'feelings of approval' they elicit, and **'utilitarians'**, who define them in terms of 'pleasure, or happiness', think so (p. 106). If 'moral judgements' could be turned into 'psychological or sociological' ones, they would not be '**generically different**' from 'factual assertions', so our account of 'empirical hypotheses' would apply to them too (p. 106). However, both the subjectivist and utilitarian analyses must be rejected. It is not 'self-contradictory' to hold that actions or things which are 'generally approved of' are not right or good, nor is it self-contradictory to say that it is sometimes wrong to 'perform the action' that would probably produce 'the greatest happiness', or the 'greatest balance of pleasure over pain': 'x is good' is not 'equivalent to "x is pleasant"' (p. 107). Thus, the 'validity of ethical judgements' is not 'empirically calculable', but is 'absolute' or 'intrinsic' (p. 107). We cannot follow subjectivists and utilitarians, and reduce 'ethical to non-ethical statements': sentences containing '**normative ethical symbols**' are not equivalent to any sort of 'empirical propositions' (pp. 107–8).

Of course, it is only 'normative ethical symbols', not '**descriptive**' ones, which cannot be defined 'in factual terms' (p. 108). The sentence, '*x* is wrong' may express disapproval of someone's behaviour, and thus be a normative 'moral judgement', or merely state society's disapproval of it, in which case it is 'descriptive' (p. 108). It may seem that, in accepting the **irreducibility** of 'normative ethical concepts' to 'empirical' ones, we are taking an '"absolutist" view of ethics', which does not treat 'statements of value' as 'empirical propositions' but relates them to '**intellectual**' **intuitions**, which are 'unverifiable' as there is no agreed 'criterion' for deciding between those that conflict (pp. 108–9). Some 'moralists' say they 'know' subjectively that their judgements are 'correct', but this does not establish their 'validity' (p. 109). Ethical statements are claimed to be 'synthetic propositions', but the '"intuitionist" theory' offers no 'relevant empirical test' of them (p. 109).

Accepting the '"absolutist" theory' of ethics would 'undermine' our argument that a 'synthetic proposition' is only 'significant' if 'empirically verifiable', and '**"naturalistic" theories**' have already been rejected (p. 109). There is a 'third theory' that is compatible with 'radical empiricism' (p. 109). The 'absolutists' are right about the unanalysability of 'fundamental ethical concepts', but this is due to their being 'pseudo-concepts': an 'ethical symbol', like 'wrong', does not add to a proposition's 'factual content' (pp. 109–10). When I say, 'You acted wrongly in stealing that money', instead of, 'You stole that money', I make no 'further statement' of fact about the act, only express 'moral disapproval of it' (p. 110). If I 'generalize' the statement to, 'Stealing money is wrong', this sentence has 'no factual meaning', and is not a proposition that can be 'true or false' (p. 110). Someone else may 'disagree', because he feels differently 'about stealing', but he cannot 'contradict me', for neither of us is making a 'factual statement' (p. 110). We are both merely expressing our '**moral sentiments**', so it is pointless to ask which of us is 'right' (pp. 110–11). Whenever one makes 'an ethical judgement', the 'ethical word' has a 'purely **"emotive"**' function, expressing feelings about 'certain objects', but making no factual 'assertion' about them (p. 111).

As well as expressing feelings, ethical symbols also 'arouse' them and 'stimulate action'; they can also, as in the sentence, 'You ought to tell the truth', function as commands (p. 111). Indeed, the 'meaning' of such different 'ethical words' as 'good' or '**duty**' may be defined in terms of the 'different' feelings and 'responses' they are 'ordinarily taken to express' and are intended to arouse (p. 111). The reason why no criterion

57

for deciding the 'validity of ethical judgements' can be found is that they 'do not express genuine propositions', and are not 'true or false', but simply express feelings (p. 112). So, our ethical theory differs from that of 'orthodox' subjectivists, who hold that ethical judgements express 'propositions about the speaker's feelings', which would make them 'empirically verifiable', as their truth or falsity would depend on the speaker's having or not having 'the relevant feelings' (p. 112). But, 'our theory' does not regard such judgements as stating anything about 'my own feelings' or 'anything else', but just expressing them; and, although having a 'certain feeling' generally goes with expressing it, this is not always the case (pp. 112–13). So, while the 'subjectivist' holds that 'ethical statements' assert the 'existence of certain feelings', we say they express and excite them, but do not 'necessarily involve any assertions' (p. 113). Our theory thus escapes a common objection to the ordinary subjectivist theory, by avoiding the implication that the existence of certain feelings is a '**necessary and sufficient condition**' of an ethical judgement's validity (p. 113).

Moore has argued that, if 'ethical statements' are just about 'the speaker's feelings', we would not be able to 'argue about questions of value' (pp. 113–14). If, when one person says that 'thrift' is 'a virtue', and another that it is not, they are simply expressing approval or disapproval, both statements can be true (p. 114). Moore concludes that, as there are disputes about 'questions of value', subjectivism is false (p. 114). Now, it is true that the impossibility of disputing 'questions of value' does follow from our theory, but Moore's argument does not even refute the 'ordinary subjectivist theory', as no one actually disputes questions of value (p. 114). In all cases where this appears to be so, the actual dispute is about a matter of fact. When two people differ about the 'moral value of a certain action', one does not try to prove that the other has the '"wrong" ethical feeling' about it, but that he is wrong about 'the facts', through misunderstanding, or overlooking, some aspect of it, such as the 'agent's motive' or the action's effects (pp. 114–15). He hopes that agreement about the 'empirical facts' will lead his opponent to 'adopt the same moral attitude' (p. 115). But if, due to a different 'moral education', he still does not agree, the attempt to convince him is abandoned, on the ground that he has a different, and inferior, '**set of values**' (p. 115). It is because 'argument fails' in relation to questions of value that such disputes often end in 'mere abuse' (p. 115). Argument is only possible 'on moral questions' if there is a common 'system of values' (p. 115). We cannot argue about the 'validity' of another person's 'moral principles', only 'praise or condemn them', in the 'light' of ours (p. 116). Those who disagree should try to 'construct' an 'imaginary argument' about a 'question of value' which does not turn into one about a matter of 'logic' or 'empirical' fact (p. 116).

So, 'ethical philosophy' is just saying that 'ethical concepts' are '**pseudo-concepts**' and 'unanalysable'; and the job of describing the 'different feelings' they express belongs to the 'psychologist' (p. 116). There is no way to determine any ethical system's 'validity'; it is for the social scientist and psychologist to ask about the 'moral habits' of groups or individuals, and why they have them (pp. 116–17). As to '**casuistry**', it is merely 'analytical investigation' of a particular 'moral system' (p. 117). Psychological enquiry can account for both '**Kantian** and **hedonistic**' **moral theories** (p. 117). Major causes of 'moral behaviour' are fear of God's 'displeasure' and society's disapproval, which is why many regard '**moral precepts**' as '"**categorical**" commands' (p. 117). Society uses '**moral sanctions**' to promote or prevent the kind of conduct that increases or diminishes general 'contentment', which is why most 'moral codes' endorse '**altruism**', but condemn '**egotism**' (p. 117). The perceived link between 'morality and happiness' is the source of both 'hedonistic' and '**eudaemonistic' moral theories**: their 'essential defect' is treating 'propositions' which refer to the 'causes and attributes' of 'ethical feelings' as if they are 'definitions of ethical concepts', and not accepting that they are 'indefinable' pseudo-concepts (pp. 117–18).

'Aesthetic terms' are used like 'ethical' ones, and so 'aesthetic judgements' also lack 'objective validity' (p. 118). The 'purpose of aesthetic criticism' is not to 'give knowledge', but to 'communicate emotion': the critic expresses 'his own feelings' about a work of art, and tries to persuade others to 'share' them (p. 118). Thus, like ethics, aesthetics does not embody 'a unique type of knowledge' (p. 118). The only 'information' we derive from studying these 'experiences' concerns our own 'mental and physical make-up' (pp. 118–19). We cannot use 'ethical and aesthetic concepts' to construct a 'metaphysical theory' about a 'world of values', distinct from that of 'facts'; and they certainly cannot, as 'Kant hoped', provide the basis for establishing the 'existence of a transcendent god' (p. 119).

What of 'religious knowledge' (p. 119)? The existence of a 'being' with the 'attributes' that define 'the god of any **non-animistic religion**' is not '**demonstratively certain**' (p. 119). Only '*a priori* propositions' are 'logically certain': 'empirical' ones are just 'probable' (p. 119). God's existence cannot be deduced from the former because they are 'tautologies', from which only others 'can be validly deduced' (pp. 119–20). Further, the existence of, for example, the '**God of Christianity**' cannot be proved to be 'even probable' (p. 120). It is claimed that the presence of '**regularity in nature' amounts to 'sufficient evidence' for God's existence**; but, if '"God exists" en-

tails no more' than **natural phenomena** occurring in 'certain sequences', all it says is that there is the 'requisite regularity in nature' (p. 120). And this would not satisfy those who say that God exists, as they are referring to a 'transcendent being', who may be 'known through' but cannot be 'defined in terms of those manifestations' (p. 120). 'God' is a 'metaphysical' term, so it cannot even be probable that God exists, as no 'metaphysical utterance' can be either 'true or false'; and no sentence purporting to describe a transcendent God's 'nature' can have any 'literal significance' (p. 120).

This view must not be confused with the **agnostic** one, that God's existence is 'a possibility', which there is no 'good reason' for believing or disbelieving, or the **atheist** position, that it is probable that God does not exist (pp. 120–1). Our view, that 'utterances' about **God's nature** are 'nonsensical', is 'incompatible' with both these positions (p. 121). The atheist's assertion that 'there is no god' is as 'nonsensical' as the theist's assertion that there is, while the agnostic accepts that sentences affirming the existence or non-existence of a 'transcendent' God express 'propositions' that are either true or false (p. 121). We hold that such sentences do not 'express propositions', so both the theist and 'the moralist' can find the 'same comfort' in their 'assertions' being neither 'valid' nor 'invalid'; they say 'nothing' about 'the world', so cannot be 'false' (p. 121). Those who identify their gods with 'natural objects', such as 'thunder', do make 'significant' assertions about them, but, in **'sophisticated religions'**, the 'person' believed to 'control the empirical world' is held to be 'superior to' and 'outside it', and to have 'super-empirical attributes'; but this is not an **'intelligible notion'** (pp. 121–2). The existence of the 'word "god"' fosters 'the illusion' that a 'real', or at least 'possible', 'entity' corresponds to it, but when we investigate

'**God's attributes**', we find that 'God' is 'not a genuine name' (p. 122). Belief in 'an **after-life**' often accompanies belief in God, and, while a statement to the effect that people never die would be a 'significant proposition', though contrary to all 'available evidence', saying that there is a '**soul**' or 'real self' inside human beings is a 'metaphysical assertion' that lacks 'factual content' (p. 122).

Our account of 'religious assertions' means there is no 'logical ground' for conflict between 'religion and natural science', for the theist's 'utterances' are not 'genuine propositions' (pp. 122–3). The 'antagonism' between the two seems to arise from the fact that science removes one of the reasons that make people 'religious': being unable to 'determine their own destiny' (p. 123). Science enables us to understand, and to a degree control, 'natural phenomena' (p. 123). But it is not part of this book to discuss 'the causes of religious feeling': what we want to establish is that there can be no 'transcendent truths of religion', as the sentences used to express them are not 'literally significant' (p. 123). And this is what theists themselves think. They hold that God's nature 'transcends' human 'understanding', making it 'unintelligible' and incapable of being 'significantly' described (p. 124). It is also said that God is not 'an object of reason', but 'of faith' (p. 124). However, if this means that God is an 'object of a **purely mystical intuition**', he cannot be defined in terms that are 'intelligible to the reason', and so no sentence can be both 'significant' and 'about God' (p. 124).

The 'mystic' may contend that intuition discloses 'truths' that cannot be explained to others (p. 124). We do not deny that 'synthetic' truths may be discovered by 'purely intuitive methods', as well as by 'induction', but they must be 'subject to the test of actual experience' (p. 124). If the mystic really had 'acquired any information', he would be able to 'indicate' ways of determining its 'genuineness' empirically: his inability to do so shows that mystical intuition is not a '**genuinely cognitive state**' (p. 125). This also applies to **arguments to God's existence 'from religious experience**' (p. 125). Some theists say that it is 'logically possible' for people to be 'immediately acquainted with God', as they are with sense-contents (p. 125). But the religious believer is usually also saying that there is a 'transcendent being', who is 'the object' of this experience, just as one, who says he sees a 'yellow patch', is also saying that there is a yellow object, to which his 'sense-content belongs' (pp. 125–6). However, a sentence about the existence of a yellow object can be 'empirically verified', but one about 'a transcendent god' cannot (p. 126). Arguments from religious experience do not imply that there is 'religious knowledge', any more than 'moral experience' implies there is 'moral knowledge' (p. 126). Both theists and moralists may think their 'experiences' are 'cognitive', but, unless they can express their 'knowledge' in 'empirically verifiable' propositions, they deceive themselves (p. 126).

Chapter 7
The Self and the Common World (pp. 127–43)

Writers of '**epistemological treatises**' generally assume that 'empirical knowledge' must have 'a basis of certainty', and that there must be objects that exist in a logically 'indubitable' way (p. 127). To provide empirical knowledge with the logical 'certification' they think it needs, they see their job as being not only to describe things 'immediately "given" to us', but also to offer a 'logical proof' of the existence of things that are not (p. 127). Our view is that empirical knowledge can only be justified **pragmatically**, not logically. Unless 'metaphysical objects' exist, 'sense-experiences' are the 'only proof' of things not 'immediately "given"': there is no *'a priori* proof' (p. 127). With the 'problem of perception', we had to take up a 'phenomenalist' position, in order to avoid 'metaphysics': the same is true of the problems of our 'knowledge of our own existence' and that of 'other people' (pp. 127–8).

As '**existence is not a predicate**', stating that an 'object exists' is a 'synthetic proposition', so no object's existence is beyond doubt (p. 128). Synthetic propositions, including those describing 'our sensations', however 'great their probability', are not 'logically sacrosanct' (p. 128). There is no 'logical certainty' about empirical knowledge, and one who denies a synthetic proposition, however irrational he may seem, does not 'necessarily' contradict himself (p. 128). This is not to say that sense-experience has 'no real content', only that any 'description' of it is an 'empirical hypothesis', the 'validity' of which cannot be guaranteed (p. 128). Although our 'empiricist doctrine' is a 'logical' one, concerned with distinguishing between 'analytic propositions, synthetic propositions, and metaphysical verbiage', and is 'compatible' with any 'theory' about the 'characteristics' of our 'sensory fields', it is impossible to avoid all the issues that have been raised about the 'character' of what is 'given' to us in sense-experience (p. 129). No 'empirical test' can resolve the issues of whether 'sense-contents' are 'mental or physical', 'private to a single self', or can exist 'without being experienced': the only possible 'solution' is an *'a priori'* one (p. 129).

We reject the 'realist analysis' of 'our sensations' as 'subject, act, and object' (p. 129). We do not deny the legitimacy of saying that a 'particular subject' experiences a 'given sense-content', but this must be 'analysed' in terms not of a '**substantival ego and its mysterious acts**', but of the 'relation-ship' between 'sense-contents' (pp. 129–30). A 'sense-content' is not 'the object', but 'part' of 'a sense-experience', so saying a sense-experience or content 'exists' is not the same as say-ing 'a material thing' does (p. 130). We define the latter in terms of the sense-contents that constitute it; it is a 'logical construction' out of them (p. 130). But 'a sense-experience' is a 'whole', comprised of sense-contents, and cannot be de-scribed as a 'logical construction' from them (p. 130). To pre-vent their being treated as 'material things', we should refer to 'sense-contents' and experiences as occurring, not existing (p. 130).

The 'distinction' between 'mental' and 'physical' is not ap-plicable to 'sense-contents', only to things logically constructed out of them, so when 'we distinguish' between particular 'mental' or 'physical' objects, we are distinguishing between 'different logical constructions', the 'elements' of which are neither 'mental' nor 'physical' (pp. 130–1). Of course, saying an object is a 'logical construction' out of sense-contents does not mean it is 'actually constructed' from them, or that they are 'parts of it'; it is a 'convenient' way of indicating that 'all sentences' that refer to the object are 'translatable' into ones that refer to the sense-contents (p. 131). Thus, the 'distinction between mind and matter' applies only to 'logical construc-tions', and all distinctions between the latter are 'reducible' to those between sense-contents (p. 131). Further, the 'distin-guishing feature' of what belongs to the 'category of "one's own mental states"' is that the sense-contents constituting them are mostly 'introspective', while what relates to others' 'mental states' consists of sense-contents that are 'elements of other living bodies' (p. 131). We form a 'single class of mental objects' from these 'two classes', due to the close '**qualitative**

similarity' between the 'sense-contents', relating to 'other living bodies', and those relating to our own (pp. 131–2). Further, the only 'philosophical problem' about the mind/matter 'relationship' is that of defining 'symbols' denoting 'logical constructions' in terms of those denoting 'sense-contents' (p. 132). The traditional philosophical problem of 'bridging' a 'gulf' between 'mind and matter' is 'fictitious', resulting from thinking of them as 'substances' (p. 132). Once 'metaphysics' is disposed of, any '*a priori* objections' to 'causal' or '**epistemological**' connections between 'minds and material things' dissolve: for example, to say that 'mental object M' and 'physical object X' are 'causally connected' is merely to say that, when a sense-content that is 'an element of M' occurs, this is a 'reliable' indicator of the 'occurrence' of one that is an 'element of X'; and the truth of such a proposition can be empirically verified (pp. 132–3).

Can a sense-content occur in the 'sense-history' of more than 'a single self' (p. 133)? A 'self' is a 'logical construction' from sense-experiences, and its 'nature' concerns the 'relationship' between them (p. 133). For 'any two sense-experiences' to 'belong to the sense-history of the same self', it is 'necessary and sufficient' for them to contain 'organic sense-contents' that are 'elements of the same body' (p. 133). But an 'organic sense-content' cannot, logically, be 'an element of more than one body', from which it 'follows necessarily' that the 'sense-histories of different selves' cannot have 'sense-experiences' in common (pp. 133–4). This amounts to saying that it is 'logically impossible' for a 'sense-experience' to belong to 'the sense-history of more than a single self' (p. 134). However, as a sense-content must be 'contained in a single sense-experience', if 'all sense-experiences' are 'subjective', so are 'all sense-contents' (p. 134).

This explanation of the self is at odds with the view that it is 'a substance', but, if it is, why is it 'unobservable' (p. 134)? It is not disclosed in 'self-consciousness', which is just the self's 'ability' to recall 'earlier states': in other words, some of the 'sense-experiences' constituting the particular self contain 'memory images', corresponding to 'sense-contents' that have 'occurred' before in his 'sense-history' (p. 134). A 'substantive ego' cannot be located 'anywhere', and is as 'unverifiable' and 'metaphysical' as Locke's theory of a '**material substratum**' (p. 134). The 'considerations' which led Berkeley to provide a 'phenomenalist account of material things' also require (as he failed to realize) a similar account of 'the self' (p. 135). As Hume pointed out, when probing the self, there are only perceptions, and so he concluded that the self is a mere 'bundle' of 'different perceptions', lacking any clear 'unifying principle' (p. 135). While 'self-consciousness' has to be 'defined in terms of memory', he realized that 'self-identity' cannot be: no individual can recall all the 'perceptions' he has had, yet those that cannot be recalled contribute just as much to the self as those that can (p. 135).

Rationalists have treated Hume's inability to identify a unifying principle as evidence of the inadequacy of 'empiricist' accounts 'of the self' (pp. 135–6). However, we have solved 'Hume's problem', by 'defining personal identity in terms of bodily identity' and the latter 'in terms of the resemblance and continuity of sense-contents' (p. 136). And our account is borne out by the fact that, while it is not 'self-contradictory' to refer to an individual as having survived 'memory' loss, this is not the case with bodily 'annihilation' (p. 136). Believers in an after-life are not referring to the 'empirical self', but to the 'soul', a 'metaphysical entity', logically unconnected with it (p. 136). We differ from Hume, in that he thought of the self as an 'aggregate of sense-experiences', while our position is that it is 'reducible' to them: to talk of 'the self' is to talk of 'sense-experiences' (p. 136).

Our 'thoroughgoing phenomenalism', coupled with acceptance that 'sense-experiences' are 'private' to the 'single self', will invite the response that, logically, this is a **solipsistic position**, offering 'no good reason' for believing in other people's existence; but this does not follow necessarily from 'our epistemology' (pp. 136–7). Unlike some philosophers, I am not saying that we can infer the 'probability' of other people's existence from our 'own experiences' (p. 137). We can 'legitimately' employ '**analogy**' to 'establish the probable existence' of something we have not experienced, if our experiencing it is conceivable; but this is not the case with 'other people', when 'it is assumed' that we have no access to 'their experiences', making them 'metaphysical objects' (pp. 138–9). But, in fact, the 'assumption' that others' 'experiences' are inaccessible is wrong (p. 139). Just as 'material things and my own self' are defined 'in terms of their empirical manifestations', so are other people, in terms of bodily 'behaviour', and, 'ultimately', 'sense-contents' (p. 139). My 'hypothesis' that others exist is 'verified' by the 'appropriate series of sense-contents' occurring (p. 139). Further, the 'distinction' between a 'conscious' human being and a machine is that the first satisfies, but the second does not, an 'empirical' test to determine that 'consciousness' is present (p. 140). So, here is the solution to the 'philosophical problem' of 'knowledge of other people': it is a matter of pointing out the way that a 'certain type of hypothesis' can be 'empirically verified' (p. 140).

Further, 'our phenomenalism' is consistent with our belief that human beings 'communicate' and 'inhabit a common world' (p. 141). It does not follow from the individual's 'experiences' being 'private to himself' that there is 'good reason' for believing those of others to be 'qualitatively' different from ours, because we define the 'qualitative identity and difference' of 'two people's sense-experiences' by the 'similarity and dissimilarity of their reactions to empirical tests' (p. 141). For example, to decide whether two people have 'the same colour sense', we see whether they categorize 'colour expanses' in the same way (p. 141). We all have to 'define the content' of others' sense-experiences in terms of what we can 'observe' ourselves (p. 142). If we see their experiences as 'essentially unobservable entities', the 'nature' of which we have to infer from their 'perceptible behaviour', even their existence becomes a 'metaphysical hypothesis' (p. 142). Instead, we must regard the 'content', as well as the 'structure', of others' experiences, as 'accessible': otherwise, we can make no 'significant statements' about them (p. 142). We have 'good reason' to believe that we 'understand' others, and vice versa, because of the appropriate 'effect' of our respective 'utterances' (p. 142). Thus, despite the 'private' nature of our experiences, we are entitled to hold that we 'inhabit a common world' with others; and no part of 'our epistemology' is at odds with 'this fact' (p. 143).

Chapter 8
Solutions of Outstanding Philosophical Disputes
(pp. 144–70)

One purpose of this book has been to establish that, as philosophy's 'function' is to elucidate the 'consequences' of 'our linguistic usages', there is no justification for the existence of philosophical 'schools' (p. 144). Philosophy's concern is with 'purely logical questions', and when disputes occur it is because 'one party' is 'guilty' of an error, which, if it cannot be identified, is because it is 'too subtle' (p. 144). Questions that are 'not logical' can be 'dismissed' as 'metaphysical', or subjected to 'empirical inquiry' (pp. 144–5). I shall now examine the 'three great issues', those between 'rationalists and empiricists', 'realists and idealists', and 'monists and pluralists', which have divided philosophers, to show that in each case the theses maintained by the two sides in the dispute are 'partly logical, partly metaphysical, and partly empirical' (p. 145). It is not our intention to 'vindicate' one side or the other, but to 'settle certain questions', which have played a disproportionately large part in the 'history of philosophy' (p. 145).

Rationalism and Empiricism (pp. 146–50)

'Rationalists' maintain the 'metaphysical doctrine' that there is a **'suprasensible world'**, known by 'intellectual intuition', which alone is 'wholly real' (p. 146). This is a 'senseless' doctrine, for no 'empirical observation' is relevant to establishing it (p. 146). Further, the rationalists are wrong to think that there are '*a priori* propositions', referring to 'matters of fact', but so are those 'empiricists' who hold that all 'significant propositions' are 'empirical' (p. 146). There are 'necessarily valid' *a priori* propositions, which are not, as the rationalists believe, 'speculative "truths of reason"', but 'tautologies' (p. 146). Thus, rejecting 'metaphysics' does not involve denial that there are 'necessary truths' (p. 147).

We cannot accept the positivists' 'criterion' for distinguishing between a 'metaphysical utterance' and a 'genuine synthetic proposition', that the latter be 'conclusively verifiable': no synthetic proposition can be more than 'highly probable' (p. 147). We take instead a 'weakened' form of the 'verification principle', and consider a proposition 'genuinely factual', if 'any empirical observations' are 'relevant to its truth or falsehood' (p. 147). We also reject the 'positivist doctrine' that 'symbols', apart from '**logical constants**', must stand for 'sense-contents', or be 'explicitly definable' in terms of ones that do (pp. 147–8). We maintain that symbols can be legitimately used, if it can be indicated how the propositions that they help 'to express may be empirically substantiated' (p. 148).

We do not necessarily embrace any particular 'doctrines' put forward by 'empirical authors' (p. 148). For example, we accept Hume's views about the 'validity of general propositions of law', but not that all 'general' hypotheses are generalizations from 'a number of observed instances'; scientists do not just 'wait' for 'nature to instruct' them (pp. 148–9). Rather, we side with 'the rationalists': scientists sometimes consider a law's 'possibility' before they have 'the evidence' that 'justifies it', and use 'deductive reasoning' to determine what, if their 'hypothesis' is correct, they should 'experience in a given situation' (p. 149). 'Theorizing' is a 'creative activity' in which the 'mind' takes an active part: but we must be careful to distinguish the 'psychological question', about how knowledge originates, from the 'logical' one, about its certification (pp. 149–50). What the rationalists say about the role of intuition in acquiring 'knowledge' is 'probably true', but it cannot (as in the case of 'scientific laws') be 'intuitively validated' (pp. 149–50).

Realism and Idealism (pp. 150–61)

The 'realist-idealist controversy' becomes 'metaphysical' when 'the question' of an object's being 'real or ideal' is seen as an 'empirical' one, which (unlike the usual situation of its being 'real', as 'opposed' to 'illusory') no 'possible observation' can resolve, as it concerns the 'fictitious' issue of whether it has the 'completely undetectable' properties of being 'real' or 'ideal' (pp. 150–1). 'Berkeleyan idealists' hold that *'x* is real', or 'exists', is 'equivalent' to *'x* is perceived', so it is 'self-contradictory' to state that 'anything exists unperceived', while its being perceived 'entails' its being 'mental', making 'everything that exists' mental (p. 151). The 'realists' contend that the 'concept of reality' is 'unanalysable', so 'no sentence', referring to 'perceptions', is 'equivalent' to *'x* is real' (p. 151). What 'the realists' deny is 'right', but not what 'they affirm' (p. 151). Berkeley maintained that material things cannot 'exist unperceived', because they are no more than their 'sensible qualities', which qualities it would be 'self-contradictory' to say 'existed unsensed' (p. 151). However, he did not reject the 'common-sense' view that objects exist when people are not perceiving them: they can 'still be perceived by God', which proves the 'existence of a personal god' (pp. 151–2).

'Berkeley's reasoning' is clearly erroneous (p. 152). Realists say he fails to 'distinguish' the 'object sensed' from the 'act of consciousness' aimed at it, and that it is not self-contradictory to say that the former exists 'independently of the act' (p. 152). But I think Berkeley was 'right' to regard the 'ideas' of 'sense-experience' as 'the contents', not the 'objects of sensations', and was thus correct to maintain that a 'sensible quality' cannot 'exist unsensed' (p. 153). His 'dictum, *"Esse est percipi"*', is true of 'sense-contents': saying they exist is just saying they occur, and it is self-contradictory to say they occur 'without being experienced' (p. 153). His error was to misconceive the 'relationship' between 'material things' and the 'sense-contents' that 'constitute them' (p. 153). The latter are not 'parts' of material things, as these are 'logical' constructions from them

(p. 153). And this is a 'linguistic proposition', stating that to say anything about a material thing is 'equivalent' to saying 'something' about sense-contents (p. 153). A material thing can exist, without being 'experienced', if it is 'capable of being experienced': as Mill put it, a material thing is 'a permanent possibility of sensation' (p. 154). Thus, we do not need God's 'perceptions', while we can say that people exist in the same way that material things do: the individual's 'own existence', that of others and 'material things' are to be defined 'in terms of the hypothetical occurrence of sense-contents' (pp. 154–5).

The 'immediate data of sense' are not 'necessarily mental', nor are things just the 'sum' of their 'sensible qualities': they are 'logical constructions' out of 'sense-contents', and the terms 'physical' and 'mental' apply just to 'logical constructions'; it cannot 'significantly' be said that sense-contents are, or are not, 'mental' (p. 155). The belief that they are derives from Descartes, who, holding that 'his own existence' could be derived from 'a thought', considered the 'mind' to be 'a substance', 'wholly independent' of the 'physical', and capable of experiencing only 'what belonged to itself' (p. 155). But this is a 'metaphysical' view (p. 156). Descartes' use of 'thought' to indicate a 'single introspective sense-content' means it is not 'mental' in the usual 'usage'; and, even if a 'conscious' being's existence could be deduced from a single 'mental datum', this would not rule out that being's having 'direct causal and epistemological relations' with 'material things': in fact, there are strong 'empirical grounds' for rejecting the complete independence of 'mind and matter' (p. 156). The 'argument from illusion' (that material things look different, depending on where they are observed from) is cited in support of the doctrine that we 'directly' experience only 'what is mental': but all this proves is that 'sense-content' is not related to 'material thing' as 'part

73

to whole' (p. 156). Berkeley also argued that all 'sensations' involve pleasure or pain, with which, as they cannot be distinguished 'phenomenally' from them, they must be 'identified'; and, as these are undoubtedly 'mental', so, too, are the 'objects of sense' (p. 157). But, apart from specific ones (as 'in my shoulder'), 'pains and pleasures' refer to 'logical constructions', and not to 'sense-contents', which are not 'mental' or 'physical' (p. 157).

Many non-Berkeleyan 'idealists' maintain that saying something 'is real' is 'equivalent to' its being 'thought of', making it 'self-contradictory' to maintain that a thing 'exists unthought of', or that a thought-of thing is 'unreal' (p. 157). However, just because judging something to exist 'entails' its being 'thought of', this does not make it 'self-contradictory' to hold that an 'unthought of' thing exists: it may exist without ever being thought of (p. 158). The belief that what is thought of 'must necessarily be real' derives from the erroneous 'assumption' that sentences like 'Unicorns are thought of' have the 'same logical form' as 'Lions are killed' (p. 158). But, unlike 'being killed', 'being thought of' is not 'an attribute'; therefore, there is no self-contradiction in holding that things that are thought of 'do not actually exist' (p. 158). Further, even if there were an equivalence between being 'real' and being 'thought of', this would not justify the idealist view that 'everything that exists is mental': no 'empirical ground' exists for adopting the view that what we have always regarded as 'material things' are actually 'conscious' (p. 159).

It is not 'self-contradictory' to hold that things exist 'unperceived': but are the 'realists' right that we have 'good reason' to think that they 'continue to exist', when not perceived (p. 159)? There is 'good inductive ground' for this view (p. 159). When we say a thing exists unperceived, we are saying that 'certain

sense-contents would occur', given fulfilment of 'certain conditions' (pp. 159–60). The fact that I now perceive 'a table'
and other 'material things', have always 'perceived' them,
and have observed others doing so, is a 'good inductive basis'
for the 'generalization' that, in 'such circumstances', 'these
material things always are perceptible', even if, at particular
times, no one may 'actually' be doing so; and thus for believing that material things exist unperceived (p. 160). There are
also 'good inductive grounds' for holding that things exist
that have actually never 'been perceived' (pp. 160–1).

Monism and Pluralism (pp. 161–70)

No 'empirical situation' is relevant to the monists' claim
(denied by realists) that '**Reality is One**': it is a 'metaphysical
assertion', arising from 'logical errors' (p. 161). Monists believe that stating 'any fact about a thing' is to state 'every fact
about everything', amounting to the view that 'any true proposition' can be deduced from any other, and from this 'it follows' that 'any two sentences' that express 'true propositions
are equivalent' (p. 162). As monists use '"truth" and "reality"
interchangeably', this leads to the 'metaphysical assertion' that
'Reality is One' (p. 162). They accept that the actual sentences
people use are not 'equivalent' to each other, but hold that this
just shows that 'none of the propositions' a person believes is
actually 'true' (p. 162).

The monists' 'paradoxical conclusions' arise from a 'crucial'
false 'step' in their argument: that all a thing's 'properties',
including its 'relational' ones, are 'constitutive of its nature'
(p. 162). Of course, the word 'nature' is ambiguous in this
context: it could mean that all a thing's 'properties' are 'relevant to its behaviour', or that they are 'defining properties' of

it; but only from the second would it 'follow' that 'every fact' about a particular thing was 'logically deducible from every other' (p. 162–3). But to attribute to something a 'property' that 'belongs to it by definition' is to state a 'tautology', so, if all a thing's 'properties' are 'constitutive of its nature', the 'absurd' result would be that no 'synthetic fact' could be stated about it (p. 163). However, this 'false' view gains plausibility from the 'ambiguity' of a sentence like: If this object lacked 'the properties which it has, it would not be what it is' (p. 163). This could be an 'analytic proposition', stating that a thing cannot both have, and lack, a particular 'property'; but this does not mean that all its 'properties' are 'defining' ones (pp. 163–4). For example, while it is 'self-contradictory' to say there is no 'news' in 'my newspaper', there is none in saying that it is not on this 'table' (p. 164). One problem is that a 'predicate', which, with one 'descriptive phrase' expresses an 'analytic' proposition, may when put with another express a 'synthetic' one, despite referring to 'the same object': for example, 'the author of *Hamlet* wrote *Hamlet*' is 'analytic', but 'Shakespeare wrote *Hamlet*' is 'synthetic' (pp. 164–5).

As well as 'every fact' being 'logically contained' in 'every other', monists generally also maintain that 'every event' is 'causally connected with every other' (p. 165). But 'causality' is not a 'logical relation' (p. 165). If it were, the 'contradictory' of every 'true proposition', stating a 'causal connexion', would be 'self-contradictory'; but, as Hume showed, such propositions concern 'matters of fact', and are 'synthetic', so their 'validity' cannot be 'established *a priori*' (pp. 165–6). There are 'good empirical grounds' for not accepting the view that 'every event' is 'causally connected with every other': it would rule out 'natural science', by making all 'data' relevant to every scientific 'prediction', so that it would be impossible to make them, as we would always be 'ignoring' a lot of 'relevant data' (pp. 166–7). However, many scientific predictions are 'successful', vindicating our 'judgements' that much data is irrelevant, and showing that the 'monistic doctrine' is wrong (p. 167).

We must reveal monism's 'errors', as we want to 'uphold the unity of science', recognition of which is currently hindered by needless 'multiplicity' of 'scientific terminologies' (p. 167). Even more important is philosophy's 'unity' with science, with which it does not compete as its propositions are 'purely linguistic' (p. 168). The philosopher's role is to elucidate 'scientific theory', by 'defining' its 'symbols'; and **Einstein**'s work highlights the importance of 'clear and definitive analyses of the concepts' for 'experimental' physics (p. 168). Again, a major reason why **psychology and psycho-analysis** cannot free themselves from 'metaphysics' is imprecise definition of terms like 'intelligence' and 'subconscious self' (pp. 168–9). 'Philosophical elucidation' of 'their symbols' is needed, so that their 'real empirical content' can be clearly identified (p. 169).

Further, 'without science', philosophy is 'virtually empty' (p. 169). Analysing 'everyday language' pinpoints, and removes, some 'metaphysics', but these problems will soon be solved: most, including 'perception', the hardest, are covered in 'this book' (p. 169). The philosopher's role is to clarify 'contemporary' scientific 'concepts', but he must 'understand science' to do so (p. 169). It is helpful to distinguish between the 'speculative' and 'logical aspects of science': philosophy must become the 'logic of science', with the philosopher making clear the 'logical relationship' between scientific 'hypotheses' and 'defining the symbols' that occur in them (p. 170).

Detailed Summary of Ayer's Language, Truth and Logic

Overview

The following section is a chapter-by-chapter overview of the eight chapters in A. J. Ayer's *Language, Truth and Logic*, designed for quick reference to the Detailed Summary above. Readers may also find this section helpful for revision.

Preface to First Edition (pp. 9–11)

Ayer explains that his views derive from Russell, Wittgenstein, Berkeley and Hume. He accepts the latter's division of genuine propositions into the *a priori* ones of logic and pure mathematics, which are necessary, because analytic, and those about matters of fact, which are probable, but not certain. He uses a modified verification principle to test whether a sentence contains a genuine empirical hypothesis: it need not be conclusively verifiable, but a possible sense-experience must be relevant to its truth or falsity. If not, and it is not analytic either, it is metaphysical and literally senseless. This criterion shows a lot, thought to be philosophy, such as God's existence and a non-empirical world of values, to be metaphysical.

Philosophy can offer neither speculative truths, to compete with scientific hypotheses, nor *a priori* judgements about the validity of scientific theories; it can only clarify its propositions. This removes any justification for rival philosophical schools, and he will solve traditional philosophical problems. The view that philosophy is an analytical activity is associated with Moore, who does not share Ayer's thoroughgoing phenomenalism. His views are closest to those of logical positivists like Schlick and Carnap; he is also indebted to Gilbert Ryle and Isaiah Berlin.

Chapter 1
The Elimination of Metaphysics (pp. 13–29)

Ayer maintains that traditional philosophical disputes are unjustified, and can be ended by establishing the nature of philosophical enquiry. The metaphysical thesis, that philosophy gives knowledge of a reality that transcends the world of science and common sense, is wrong; those who believe in one should be asked about the premises from which they deduce their propositions. They must begin with the evidence of the senses, but, as nothing super-empirical can legitimately be inferred from empirical premises, they cannot reach a transcendent reality. The metaphysician may claim that a faculty of intellectual intuition gives him access to facts that cannot be known from sense-experience, but, as no proposition referring to a transcendent reality can have literal significance, it must be nonsense. Kant criticized metaphysics on the grounds that human understanding cannot go outside the phenomenal world, but Ayer's position is that it is fruitless to try to go beyond possible sense-experience, because of the rule determining language's literal significance: the metaphysician's sentences do not comply with its conditions. Verifiability is the criterion for testing whether a sentence expresses a genuine proposition about a matter of fact. A sentence is only factually significant if it is known what observations are relevant to determining its truth or falsity: otherwise, it is a pseudo-proposition.

Practical verifiability and verifiability in principle must be distinguished. There are significant propositions about matters of fact which there are no practical means of verifying, but it is known what observations would decide their truth, so they are verifiable in principle; but no conceivable observation could determine the truth or falsity of a metaphysical pseudo-proposition. The distinction between the strong and weak senses of verifiability is important. The first is when a proposition's truth can be conclusively verified in experience, the second when there is the possibility of experience making it probable. As general propositions, such as 'All men are mortal', cannot be established with certainty by any finite series of observations, making conclusive verifiability the criterion of significance would mean treating them like metaphysical statements, so it would be impossible to make any significant factual statements. Limiting factually significant sentences to those confutable by experience would be just as bad: it is no more possible to confute than to verify a hypothesis conclusively.

The weaker sense of verification must be adopted. Of any supposed statement of fact, it must be asked whether any observations are relevant to determining its truth or falsehood: it is only nonsensical if they are not. The mark of a genuine factual proposition is not that it should be equivalent to a proposition that records an actual or possible observation, but that such propositions can be deduced from it, together with certain other premises, which could not be deduced from those other premises alone. This criterion would rule out as nonsensical an assertion like, 'The world of sense-experience is unreal.' The senses may deceive people at times, but it is further sense-experience that brings the mistakes to light. No conceivable observation could show that the world, revealed to us by sense-experience, is unreal, and any statement that it is mere appearance is literally nonsensical. So, no possible observation is relevant to, for example, solving the dispute between monists, who say reality is one substance, and pluralists, who say it is many: neither assertion is significant. The same is true of the realist-idealist controversy. No process

exists for determining whether something is real, as opposed
to ideal.

Philosophy must be distinguished from metaphysics. Historically, a lot of what has passed for philosophy has been
metaphysical, but most great philosophers were not metaphysicians. Further, all propositions with factual content are
empirical hypotheses, whose function is to give a rule for anticipating experience, and they must relate to some actual, or
possible experience. Metaphysical utterances are nonsensical,
because they lack factual content, and are not *a priori* propositions (which are certain, because they are tautologies) either.
All significant propositions belong to one of these two classes.
The term 'substance' illustrates how a lot of metaphysics
arises. A thing's sensible properties can only be referred to in
language that seems to stand for the thing itself, as distinct
from what is said about it. Those who believe that there must
be a single real entity, corresponding to every name, then
maintain that the thing itself must be distinguished from
its sensible properties, and use the term 'substance' to refer
to the former. Logical analysis shows that what makes them
appearances of the same thing is their relationship to each
other, not to an entity other than themselves.

Again, sentences expressing existential and attributive
propositions may have the same grammatical form, and be
assumed to be of the same logical type. 'Martyrs exist' may
be thought to credit this group with an 'attribute', in the same
way 'martyrs suffer' does, since both have a noun and an intransitive verb. But Kant has shown that existence is not an
attribute: if it were, positive existential propositions would be
tautological, and negative ones self-contradictory, which is not
the case. A similar mistake arises from the superficial grammatical resemblance between 'unicorns are fictitious' and

'dogs are faithful'. It is argued that, to be fictitious, unicorns must exist, but, as it is self-contradictory to maintain that fictitious objects exist, they exist in some non-empirical sense. This assertion lacks literal significance, as there is no way of testing it. It is made because of the assumption that being fictitious is an attribute.

It is easy to write literally nonsensical sentences, and many traditional philosophical problems are metaphysical and fictitious. Metaphysicians may be seen as poets, but most poetry has literal meaning. The metaphysician does not mean to write nonsense; he is deceived into it by grammar or reasoning errors. Some metaphysical passages express genuine mystical feeling, but they are literally senseless and irrelevant to philosophy.

Chapter 2
The Function of Philosophy (pp. 30–47)

For Ayer, abandoning metaphysics frees philosophy from trying to build a deductive system of first principles, which gives a complete picture of reality. There are no first principles that can be a certain basis of knowledge: the laws of nature are just hypotheses, confutable by experience. But philosophical system-builders prefer to base their systems on what they consider logically certain principles, rather than inductive ones. Descartes tried to derive all human knowledge from propositions that it would be self-contradictory to deny, and thought his '*cogito*' (to be interpreted as 'there is a thought now') was one. But not only does '*non cogito*' not negate itself (no significant proposition can), but his initial principle, '*cogito ergo sum*', is false. The individual's existence does not follow from there being a thought. A thought occurring at a particular time does not entail a series, sufficient to constitute a single self. Hume showed that no event intrinsically points to another, so trying to base a deductive system on propositions that describe the immediately given inevitably fails.

A priori truths cannot be the first principles. They are tautologies, from which only other ones can be validly deduced, and it would be absurd to hold that they constituted the whole truth about the universe. Believing that philosophy's role is to locate first principles, is connected to the view that its concern is study of reality as a whole; and if this means that the philosopher can stand outside the world, to get an overview of it, it is a metaphysical notion. If it means that philosophy is concerned with the content of the sciences, it is a partial truth, but it is a delusion that philosophy gives access to otherwise unattainable objects of knowledge. In principle, no form of speculative knowledge is outside the range of empirical science.

Philosophy's critical activity is not testing the validity of scientific hypotheses or everyday assumptions, but pointing out criteria for determining the truth or falsity of propositions. Empirical verification is the only possible or necessary justification for empirical propositions; and recognizing this may lead a sceptic to accept that his original beliefs are justified. We must stop insisting that science lacks logical respectability until philosophers have solved the problem of induction: that is, identified a means of proving that empirical generalizations, based on past experience, will apply in the future. The two ways of tackling this so-called problem cannot solve it. Trying to deduce it from a purely formal principle involves the mistake of thinking that a proposition about a matter of fact can be deduced from a tautology, while trying to deduce it from an empirical principle would involve assuming the truth of what needs to be proved. Induction cannot be justified on the grounds of the uniformity of nature, as this assumes the reliability of past experience as a guide to the future.

The so-called problem of induction is fictitious. Apart from self-consistency, success in making possible prediction of future experience is the only relevant test of a scientific procedure. It is an error to seek a logical guarantee that this will continue in the future. Regrettably, philosophers, interested in the so-called theory of knowledge, think that belief in material things is unjustified without a satisfactory analysis of perception. But what justifies it is having certain sensations: sense-experience is the sole basis of the validity of perceptual judgements. Philosophers should not dismiss common sense beliefs; only criticize unreflecting analysis of them. Many problems related to perception concern the metaphysical notion of substance, and the impossibility of referring to something without seeming to distinguish it generically from its qualities and states. The philosopher must not seek speculative truths or first principles, but clarification and analysis.

Enquiry into philosophy's function is intended to find a definition consistent with the practice of those regarded as philosophers, and the view that philosophy is a special branch of knowledge. Metaphysics does not meet the second condition. Philosophy's history is not just that of metaphysics; most great philosophers were analysts. Locke's approach is analytic, and does not attempt *a priori* justification of common sense beliefs, only analysis of them. Berkeley is not a metaphysician, as he denied, not material things' reality, but the adequacy of Locke's analysis of the notion of them. He realized they must be defined in terms of sense-contents, but the word 'idea', to denote what is given in sensation, misled him into thinking that it is necessarily mental. Berkeley is right that material things must be defined in terms of sense-contents, as it is only through the latter's occurrence that the former's existence can be verified. The question that has to be answered is not whether a phenomenalist theory of perception is true, but only what form it takes.

Hume rejected metaphysics. His writings are analytical, although this is sometimes challenged, due to his attempts to define causation being misinterpreted as denial of it. While his actual definitions must be rejected, he is essentially right about the nature of causation: asserting a particular causal connection involves asserting a causal law, and general propositions of the type 'C causes E', are equivalent to propositions of the type 'whenever C, then E', with the 'whenever' referring, not to a finite number of actual instances, but to the infinite number of possible ones. He is also right that success in practice is the only justification for inductive reasoning.

Hobbes and Bentham were mainly concerned with giving definitions; Mill's best work was developing Hume's analyses; and Plato, Aristotle and Kant were also mainly concerned with analysis. But, this definition of philosophy would still be right, even if no philosophers fitted it. Philosophical analysis does not depend on any metaphysical, or even empirical, presupposition about the nature of things, as it concerns, not an object's physical properties, but how it is spoken about. Philosophical propositions are linguistic, not factual, and express definitions. Philosophy is a department of logic, and, as its propositions differ in type from scientific ones, cannot contradict them. The problem is that their form of expression can make linguistic propositions look like factual ones. The statement that a material thing cannot be in two places at once looks like an empirical proposition, which leads people to think that empirical propositions can be logically certain. But, it is a linguistic proposition, which does not indicate certain knowledge of objects' empirical properties. The use of factual language must not be interpreted as showing that philosophy is an empirical or metaphysical enquiry. When the philosopher refers to analysis of facts, or notions, he refers to the definitions of the corresponding words.

Chapter 3
The Nature of Philosophical Analysis (pp. 48–63)

Philosophy's concern is not with explicit definitions, but definitions in use. The former provides another symbol, synonymous with the first, as with 'oculist' and 'eye-doctor'; the second shows how sentences in which the symbol significantly occurs can be translated into equivalent sentences, containing neither the word to be defined nor any of its synonyms. Russell's theory of definite descriptions states that all sentences containing this form of symbolic expression can be translated into ones that do not, but which do have a sub-sentence, asserting that one, and only one object possesses a certain property, or that no object possesses it. Thus, 'The round square cannot exist' is equivalent to 'No one thing can be both square and round', while, 'The author of *Waverley* was Scotch' becomes 'One person, and one person only, wrote *Waverley*, and that person was Scotch'. The first shows how to eliminate any definite descriptive phrase that is the subject of a negative existential sentence, the second how to do so with any definite descriptive phrase that occurs anywhere in any other type of sentence. They show how to express what is expressed by any sentence that contains a definite descriptive phrase, without using such a phrase, and so give a definition of these phrases in use.

Exposing their logical complexity makes it possible to understand certain sentences better. The role of philosophical definitions is to dispel confusions arising from inadequate understanding of certain types of sentence, where this cannot be done by substituting a synonym for any symbol, either because none exists, or because the synonym is unclear for the same reasons as the symbol. One complication is that many symbols, such as 'is', are ambiguous, consisting of signs that are identical in their sensible form with one another, or with signs from another symbol. It might be assumed, for example, that the 'is' in 'He is the book's author', is the same as that in 'A cat is a mammal'. However, the first sentence is equivalent to, 'He, and no one else, wrote that book', the second to, 'The class of mammals contains the class of cats'.

Saying a symbol is constituted by signs that are identical in their sensible form and significance, and that a sign is a sense-content, used to convey literal meaning, is not to say that a symbol is a collection of sense-contents. Referring to certain objects (*b, c, d*) as elements of another (*e*), is not saying they are part of it, but that sentences in which the symbol *e* occurs can be translated into ones in which it does not, but *b, c, d* do. It is a logical construction from them, and the symbols that denote logical constructions make it possible to state complicated propositions about the latter relatively simply. Logical constructions are not fictitious objects, but linguistic assertions, to the effect that a particular symbol can be defined in terms of certain symbols that stand for sense-contents, not explicitly, but in use. A sentence containing the symbol 'table' can be translated into one in which that symbol does not occur, but in which certain symbols, standing for sense-contents, do.

The problem of devising a rule for translating sentences about material things into ones about sense-contents is the principal element in the problem of perception. Philosophers who try to describe material things' nature think they are tackling a factual question, but it is to do with definitions: with the relationship of symbols, not with the properties of the things, denoted by the symbols. However, as it is not possible to describe the properties of sense-contents precisely, it is convenient to express the solution of the problem of perception in factual terminology. Material things are said to be constructed out of sense-contents, and showing the principles of this construction indicates their relationship. Questions about a material thing's nature are answered by indicating the relations that need to obtain between any two of our sense-contents for them to be elements of the same material thing.

The solution of the problem of perception illustrates the method of philosophical analysis. Two sense-contents can be said to resemble each other directly when differing only minutely in quality; indirectly, when connected by a series of direct resemblances, but not directly resemblant. Two visual, or tactual, sense-contents are directly continuous when they belong to successive members of a series of actual, or possible sense-fields, and, at most, the position of each, in its own sense-field, differs only minutely; indirectly, when related by an actual, or possible, series of such direct continuities. Saying sense-experiences, fields or contents are possible, rather than actual, is not saying they have (or will) occurred, but would under specifiable conditions. Any two of our visual or tactual sense-contents may be said to be elements of the same material object, if linked by relations of certain kinds of direct, or indirect, resemblance and continuity. The groups of visual and tactual sense-contents, constituted by these relations, cannot have members in common: no sense-content can be an element of more than one material thing.

Visual and sensual sense-contents are correlated thus. Any

two belong to the same material thing, when every element of the visual group that is of minimal visual depth, is part of the same sense-experience as one from the tactual group that is of minimal tactual depth. Depth can only be defined ostensively, but a sense-content has greater depth, the further it is from the observer's body. The sense-contents of taste, sound, or smell, relating to particular things, are classified by their association with tactual sense-contents: taste sense-contents are assigned to the same thing as those to which we assign the sense-contents of touch that the tongue is experiencing at the same time.

There is a rule for translating sentences, referring to things' real qualities: a certain quality is a particular thing's real quality, if it characterizes its most easily measured elements, as with the roundness of a coin. The aim of this outline of a definition of symbols that stand for material things is to help make the sentences, which refer to the latter, more understandable. People are unaware of the logical complexity of a sentence like 'This is a table', and may adopt a metaphysical belief about the existence of material substances. Philosophical definitions can dispel such confusions.

'Equivalence' is preferable to the ambiguous term, 'meaning'. Saying two sentences have the same meaning often signifies their affecting people's thoughts in the same way. But two sentences can be equivalent, by our criterion, but have very different psychological effects. Saying '*p* is a law of nature' is equivalent to, '*p* is a general hypothesis which can always be relied on'; but the word 'law' has connotations of 'orderliness' in nature. Again, it is misleading to say philosophy shows how certain symbols are actually used: it is not concerned with linguistic habits. When philosophers specify the language, to which their definitions apply, they just describe the conventions from which they are deduced, and generally these correspond to the conventions used.

Chapter 4
The A Priori (pp. 64–83)

Ayer's contention is that philosophy is a form of empiricism, raising the issue of how empiricism can explain knowledge of necessary truths. A general proposition can be verified in experience many times, but can never be logically certain, as it can be confuted in the future. However, this does not make it irrational to believe it: what is irrational is insistence on certainty, when only probability is obtainable. But logical and mathematical truths seem necessary and certain, so the empiricist must either deny that they are, or accept their lack of factual content. Otherwise, it will have to be accepted that the rationalists are right, and that there are truths that can be known independently of experience. But, if one of the alternatives above can be proved correct, it would destroy rationalism's foundations, as it claims that thought is an independent and more trustworthy source of knowledge than experience. Mill adopted the first alternative, arguing that logical and mathematical truths are not necessary or certain, but inductive generalizations, based on many supporting instances, and differing from scientific hypotheses, not in kind, but in degree of probability; but his view is not acceptable.

The best way to substantiate the view that logical and mathematical truths are necessarily true is to consider cases where such truths appear to be (but are not) confuted. If what are taken to be five pairs of objects are counted, but there are only nine, it is not concluded that '$2 \times 5 = 10$' has been proved wrong, but that counting errors have occurred. Whenever mathematical or logical truths seem in doubt, finding another explanation preserves their validity. Logical and mathematical truths are analytic propositions or tautologies, which are universally true, by not being allowed to be anything else. Kant defined an analytic proposition as one in which the predicate is contained in the concept of the subject, such that the former adds nothing to the latter; and a synthetic one as adding to the subject a predicate, not in any way thought in it. 'All bodies are extended' is an analytic proposition, whereas 'all bodies are heavy' is synthetic. But he also considered '7 + 5 = 12' to be synthetic, because 12 is not already thought in thinking of the combination of seven and five.

Kant's distinction between the two kinds of proposition lacks clarity, because he offers two criteria. He regards '7 + 5 = 12' as synthetic, because the subjective intension of it does not include 12, but 'all bodies are extended' as analytic, because of the principle of contradiction. Thus, he uses both psychological and logical criteria. Further, just because we can think of seven and five, without necessarily thinking of 12, it does not follow that it is not self-contradictory to deny that it is the sum of the first two numbers. The confusions of Kant's account can be removed by saying that the validity of an analytic proposition wholly depends on the definitions of the symbols it contains, while that of a synthetic one is decided by experience. Analytic propositions do not give information about matters of fact, and cannot be confuted by experience. But unlike metaphysical utterances, they are not senseless, for they clarify use of certain symbols.

In traditional logic, formal truths were insufficiently formalized, and seemed to be concerned with mental operations. Russell and Whitehead made it plain that formal logic is not about the properties of minds or objects, but the possibility of using logical particles to combine propositions into analytic ones, and their formal relationship, whereby one can be deduced from another. Unlike Aristotelian logic, in their system every logical truth serves as a principle of inference, and Aristotle's 'laws of thought' are not regarded as more important than other analytic propositions. The issue of whether or not mathematical propositions are reducible to propositions of formal logic can be ignored: even if they are not, they, too, are analytic propositions. The propositions of geometry might be thought to be synthetic, as they seem to concern the properties of physical space; but geometrical axioms are just definitions. Kant's view that mathematical propositions are synthetic can be rejected.

Analytic propositions record our determination to use words in a particular way. Their validity is independent of the nature of the external world, and of the nature of the human mind. Whatever linguistic conventions were used, analytic propositions would always be necessary. Thus, there is no mystery about the absolute certainty of logical and mathematical propositions, because the symbolic expressions used in them are synonymous. The ability of mathematics and logic to be interesting and surprising is due to the limitations of human reason. A being with an infinitely powerful intellect would see the implications of the definitions used immediately, but most people have to use forms of calculation, like the multiplication tables and the laws of logic, to work them out. Human error explains why logical and mathematical falsehoods occur: inventing symbolic devices, to express highly complex tautologies simply, can minimize them. Their being analytic is the only satisfactory explanation of the *a priori* necessity of logical and mathematical truths. Empiricists are right: there is no *a priori* knowledge of reality, and any truths known to be valid independently of all experience are so through lack of factual content.

Indicating how the validity of empirical propositions is determined will complete Ayer's theory of truth, but first he needs to justify the view that a theory of truth only concerns the issue of how propositions are validated, not the metaphysical question about the nature of truth. In fact, to ask what truth is, is to ask whether a particular proposition is true or false. The 'is true' in '*p* is true' is logically superfluous: '"Queen Anne is dead" is true' just states, 'Queen Anne is dead'. 'True' and 'false' merely signify assertion or denial, so there is no sense in trying to analyse the concept of 'truth'. Philosophers think there is, because the grammatical form of sentences in which 'truth' appears suggests that it stands for a genuine quality or relation. But, sentence analysis confirms that 'What is truth?' is reducible to 'What is the analysis of the sentence "*p* is true"?' Thus, questions about the 'something real' that 'truth' appears to stand for are illegitimate.

The question that needs to be answered concerns what makes propositions true or false: how they are validated. The criterion for deciding the validity of analytic propositions is inadequate for determining that of synthetic ones, which can be false, even if not self-contradictory. Some philosophers believe there is a special class of absolutely certain ostensive empirical propositions, validated by their directly recording an immediate experience. But a synthetic proposition cannot be purely ostensive: it is logically impossible to have an intelligible sentence, consisting solely of demonstrative symbols. Linguistically, something cannot be indicated but not described; and the description not only registers a sense-content, but moves beyond the immediately given, and classifies it. Propositions relating to material things are not ostensive, but refer to an infinite series of actual and possible sense-contents. For example, when something is said to be white, and this refers to a sense-content, not a material thing, it is classified as similar to other white things: which means that it is not an ostensive proposition, as this could not be legitimately doubted. Ones describing the actual contents of sense-contents are the only examples of ostensive propositions given, and if they are not ostensive, none is. The view that there are such propositions probably comes from the logical error of identifying propositions, referring to sensations, with the sensations themselves. So, empirical propositions are all hypotheses, the truth or falsity of which is determined by actual sense-experience.

Saying hypotheses are verified in experience means not just one, but a system. When a scientific law's validity is tested, by stating that if certain conditions obtain a certain observation will be made, and it is, the hypotheses asserting the existence of the conditions are also confirmed. If the expected observation is not made, it does not mean the law must be regarded as invalid: it may be concluded that the conditions were not as they seemed. The observations can be explained in a number of ways, although self-contradiction must be avoided. But, though cherished hypotheses can be retained against observations that seem to disprove them, the possibility of their being relinquished must exist, otherwise they are not genuine hypotheses, but definitions, and so analytic, not synthetic.

It can be difficult to distinguish genuine hypotheses from definitions, as with some laws of nature. If experience shows that all things of a certain type have a particular property, it often becomes a defining characteristic of them, and their having it becomes a tautology, not a synthetic generalization. 'All men are mortal' is often cited as an instance of a necessary connection, but what is necessarily connected here is the inclusion of the concept of being mortal in the concept of a man, making it a tautology, not an empirical hypothesis. Philosophers, who say it is a synthetic and necessary general proposition, are only able to do so by tacitly identifying it with the tautology. Turning general propositions into definitions makes them necessary, but no longer the original generalizations, which (as Hume pointed out) cannot be necessary, as experience may invalidate them.

Inconvenient observations are not ignored, and changes are made to the accepted system of hypotheses, despite the desire to keep it intact. The considerations that affect decisions about which hypotheses to keep or reject reflect the function of the system of hypotheses: to make possible accurate predictions of the future. Past experience guides expectations, and we accept that, if experience has indicated flaws in the system, it will probably fail again, and that it is better to alter it than to ignore the fact. Minor adjustments are preferred to major changes, but radical changes are made, if necessary. An empirical proposition's validity is tested by checking whether it discharges its intended function of anticipating experience. If it does, its probability is increased, although a future observation could still invalidate it.

References to observations increasing a proposition's probability, are not to an intrinsic property, but to greater confidence in it as a predictor of the future. All hypotheses should be dealt with uniformly and rationally, by always observing certain standards of evidence in the formation of beliefs.

Confidence in modern scientific methods derives from their working in practice, but use of different methods in the future may make them seem irrational. Saying that observations increase a hypothesis' probability is to say they add to the degree of confidence that it is rational to place in it, with a belief's rationality being defined, not by an absolute standard, but in relation to actual practice. All synthetic propositions are rules for anticipating future experience, and the fact that those referring to the past have the same hypothetical character as those referring to the present and future does not mean that the three types are not distinct. Propositions about the past are hypotheses, which give rules for predicting historical experiences that can verify them. Philosophers who disagree make the error of thinking that the past is objectively there, and real in some metaphysical sense.

Chapter 6
Critique of Ethics and Theology (pp. 104–26)

Some argue that there are two kinds of speculative knowledge: empirical fact and questions of value (ethics and aesthetics), and that statements of the latter are genuine synthetic propositions. Judgements of value must be explained in a way that fits in with empiricist principles, by showing that they are either ordinary scientific statements, or expressions of emotion that are neither true nor false. Ethical systems are not homogeneous, containing, in addition to elements of metaphysics and analyses of non-ethical concepts, definitions of ethical terms and judgements about their legitimacy; descriptions of the phenomena of moral experience and their causes; exhortations to moral virtue; and actual ethical judgements. Propositions about ethical terms are the whole of ethical philosophy: the other classes belong to psychology, or sociology; are commands, intended to get people to act in certain ways; or, as they are neither definitions nor comments about them, are not part of ethical philosophy. A strictly philosophical treatise on ethics should not make ethical pronouncements, but analyse ethical terms.

Subjectivists, who define goodness and rightness in terms of feelings of approval, and utilitarians, who define them in terms of pleasure or happiness, think statements of ethical value can be translated into statements of empirical fact; and, if moral judgements could be turned into psychological or sociological ones, they would not differ generically from factual assertions. Both analyses must be rejected, because it is not self-contradictory to hold that things or actions which are generally approved of are not right or good, or to say that performing the action which would probably produce the greatest happiness, is sometimes wrong: something's being good is not equivalent to its being pleasant. The validity of ethical judgements is not empirically calculable, but absolute or intrinsic: ethical statements cannot be reduced to non-ethical ones, so sentences containing normative ethical symbols are not equivalent to empirical propositions of any kind. Of course, only normative, not descriptive, ethical symbols cannot be defined in factual terms. Saying an action is wrong may be a normative moral judgement, expressing disapproval of someone's behaviour, or descriptive, saying society disapproves of it.

Accepting the irreducibility of normative ethical concepts to empirical ones may seem to endorse an absolutist theory of ethics, which treats them as unverifiable intellectual intuitions. Some moralists claim to know subjectively that their judgements are right, but this does not establish their validity.

Intuitionists claim that ethical statements are synthetic propositions, but offer no relevant empirical test. There is a theory that is compatible with radical empiricism. Fundamental ethical concepts are unanalysable, because they are pseudo-concepts: an ethical symbol, like 'wrong', does not add to a proposition's factual content. Saying someone acted wrongly in stealing money, instead of just saying he stole it, only expresses moral disapproval. The generalized statement that stealing money is wrong has no factual meaning, and cannot be true or false. Those with different feelings about stealing will disagree, but only expressions of moral sentiments, not a contradiction, are involved.

In ethical judgements, ethical words have a purely emotive function, expressing and arousing feelings, stimulating action, and functioning as commands. The reason why there is no criterion for deciding the validity of ethical judgements is that they do not express genuine propositions, and so are not true or false. This ethical theory differs from that of orthodox subjectivists, who hold that ethical judgements express propositions about the speaker's feelings, which would make them empirically verifiable. But such judgements do not state anything, but just express feelings. This theory avoids the implication that the existence of certain feelings is a necessary and sufficient condition of an ethical judgement's validity. Moore has contended that ethical statements cannot just be about feelings, as there are disputes about questions of value. However, what is actually disputed is fact. When two people differ about an action's moral value, they do not say their opponent's ethical feelings are wrong, but that he is mistaken about such facts as motives or effects. They hope agreement about the facts will change his moral attitude. If it does not, they stop trying to convince him, as he has different values. It is impossible to construct an imaginary argument about a question of value, which does not turn into one about logic or fact.

Ethical philosophy is just saying that ethical concepts are unanalysable pseudo-concepts. There is no way to determine any ethical system's validity. It is for the social scientist and psychologist to account for people having the moral habits they do. Psychological enquiry can account for both Kantian and hedonistic moral theories. Major causes of moral behaviour are fear of God's displeasure and society's enmity, which is why moral precepts are often regarded as categorical commands. Moral sanctions are used to promote or prevent behaviour that increases or diminishes society's well-being; so most moral codes endorse altruism and condemn egotism. The perceived link between morality and happiness is the source of both hedonistic and eudaimonistic theories: their defect is treating propositions which refer to the causes and attributes of ethical feelings as if they are definitions of ethical concepts. Aesthetic terms and judgements also lack objective validity: aesthetic criticism's purpose is not to give knowledge, but to communicate emotion. Ethical and aesthetic concepts cannot be used to construct a metaphysical theory about a world of values, distinct from that of facts, nor, as Kant hoped, to provide the basis for establishing God's existence.

As for religious knowledge, the impossibility of proving God's existence is demonstratively certain. Only *a priori* propositions are logically certain: empirical ones can never be more than probable. God's existence cannot be deduced from the former, because they are tautologies, from which only other tautologies can be validly deduced. It is claimed that the presence of regularity in nature is sufficient evidence of God's existence, but if saying 'God exists' entails no more than natural phenomena occurring in certain sequences, it only says that there is regularity in nature. This would not satisfy those who say God exists, as they are talking about a transcendent being, who may be known through, but cannot be defined in terms of, those manifestations. 'God' is a metaphysical term, so it cannot even be probable that God exists, as no metaphysical utterance can be either true or false.

The view that utterances about God's nature are nonsensical must not be confused with the agnostic one, that God's existence is a possibility, which there is no good reason for believing or disbelieving, or the atheist one, that God does not exist. The atheist's assertion is as nonsensical as the theist's, while the agnostic accepts that sentences affirming God's existence or non-existence express true or false propositions. In fact, they say nothing about the world, and are neither valid nor invalid. Those who identify their gods with natural objects do make significant assertions about them, but, in sophisticated religions, the person believed to control the empirical world is held to be superior to it, and to have super-empirical attributes. This is not an intelligible notion. The word 'God' fosters the illusion that a real, or possible, entity corresponds to it, but it is not a genuine name. Belief in an after-life often accompanies belief in God, and while a statement that people never die would be a significant proposition, though contrary to available evidence, saying that human beings have a soul is a metaphysical assertion, lacking factual content.

Religion and science cannot conflict, as the theist's utterances are not genuine propositions. Apparent conflict is due to science's removal of one of the reasons that make people religious: being unable to control their own destiny. But Ayer's concern is not with the causes of religious feeling. The important point is that there can be no transcendent truths of religion, as the sentences that express them are not literally significant. And this is what theists think, as they hold that God's nature transcends human understanding, which means it is incapable of being significantly described. God is also said to be an object of faith, but if this means God is an object of purely mystical intuition, he cannot be defined in intelligible terms, so no sentence can be both significant and about God.

The mystic holds that intuition discloses truths he cannot explain. Perhaps, synthetic truths can be discovered by purely intuitive methods, but they must be subjected to the test of actual experience. If the mystic had genuine information, there would be ways (which there are not) of determining its genuineness empirically. Some theists say that it is logically possible for people to be directly acquainted with God, as they are with sense-contents. But the religious believer is also saying that a transcendent being is the object of this experience, just as one who says he sees a yellow patch is also saying there is a yellow object, to which his sense-content belongs. However, a sentence about the existence of a yellow object can be empirically verified, but not one about a transcendent God. Arguments from religious experience do not imply that there is religious knowledge any more than moral experience implies there is moral knowledge. Both theists and moralists may think their experiences are cognitive, but, unless they can express their knowledge in empirically verifiable propositions, they deceive themselves.

Chapter 7
The Self and the Common World (pp. 127–43)

Writers about epistemology generally assume that empirical knowledge must have a basis of certainty, and that there must be logically indubitable objects; but empirical knowledge can only be justified pragmatically, not logically. Unless there are metaphysical objects, sense-experiences are the only proof of things not immediately given. With the problem of perception, a phenomenalist standpoint had to be adopted, to avoid metaphysics. The same is true of the problems of knowledge of our own existence and that of other people. Existence is not a predicate, so stating that an object exists is a synthetic proposition, and denying it is not self-contradictory. There is no logical certainty about empirical knowledge, and no object's existence is indubitable. This does not mean that sense-experience has no real content, only that any description of it is an empirical hypothesis, whose validity cannot be guaranteed. Although the empiricist doctrine is a logical one, which distinguishes between analytic propositions, synthetic ones, and metaphysical verbiage, and is compatible with any theory about the characteristics of our sensory fields, it is impossible to avoid all the issues about the character of what is given in sense-experience. No empirical test can resolve the issues of whether sense-contents are mental or physical, private to a single self, or can exist without being experienced: the only possible solution is an *a priori* one.

The realist analysis of sensations as subject, act and object must be rejected. This does not deny the legitimacy of saying that a particular subject experiences a given sense-content, but that this must be analysed in terms, not of a substantival ego, but of the relationship between sense-contents. A sense-content is not the object, but part of a sense-experience, so saying a sense-experience or content exists is not the same as saying a material thing does. The latter is defined in terms of the sense-contents that constitute it, and is a logical construction out of them; but a sense-experience is a whole, comprised of sense-contents, and cannot be described as a logical construction from them. To prevent their being treated as material things, we should refer to sense-contents and experiences as occurring, not existing.

The distinction between mental and physical is not applicable to sense-contents, only to things logically constructed out of them. When particular mental or physical objects are distinguished, the distinction is between different logical constructions, the elements of which are neither mental nor physical. Of course, saying an object is logically constructed out of sense-contents does not mean it is actually constructed from them, or that they are parts of it. It is a convenient way of indicating that all sentences that refer to the object are translatable into ones that refer to the sense-contents. Thus, the distinction between mind and matter applies only to logical constructions, and all distinctions between the latter are reducible to those between sense-contents. Further, the distinguishing feature of what belongs to the category of the individual's own mental states is that the sense-contents constituting them are mostly introspective, while what relates to others' mental states consists of sense-contents that are elements of other living bodies. A single class of mental objects is formed from these two classes, due to the close qualitative similarity between the sense-contents relating to others, and those relating to the individual. The only philosophical problem about the mind/matter relationship is that of defining symbols denoting logical constructions in terms of those denoting sense-contents. The traditional philosophical problems about bridging a gulf between mind and matter are fictitious, resulting from thinking of them as substances. Without metaphysics, *a priori* objections to causal or epistemological connections between minds and material things dissolve. For example, saying that a mental and physical object are causally connected is merely saying that, when a sense-content that is an element of one occurs, it is a reliable indicator of the occurrence of one that is an element of the other; and the truth of such a proposition can be empirically verified.

There is the issue of whether a sense-content can occur in the sense-history of more than a single self. A self is a logical construction from sense-experiences, and its nature concerns the relationship between them. For any two sense-experiences to belong to the history of the same self, it is necessary and sufficient for them to contain organic sense-contents that are elements of the same body. But, as an organic sense-content cannot, logically, be an element of more than one body, the sense-histories of different selves cannot have sense-experiences in common. This is the same as saying that a sense-experience cannot belong to the sense-history of more than a single self. However, as a sense-content must be contained in a single sense-experience, if all sense-experiences are subjective, so are all sense-contents. This explanation of the self clashes with the view that it is a substance; but, if it is, it is hard to see why it is unobservable. It is not disclosed in self-consciousness, which is just the self's ability to recall earlier states. A substantive ego cannot be located anywhere, and is unverifiable. The considerations which led Berkeley to provide a phenomenalist account of material things also require a similar account of the self. As Hume pointed out, there are only perceptions, and he concluded that the self is a mere bundle of different perceptions, lacking a clear unifying principle. While self-consciousness has to be defined in terms of memory, he realized that self-identity could not be: no one can recall all the perceptions he has had, but they are as constitutive of the self as those he can.

Overview

Rationalists have treated Hume's inability to identify a unifying principle as indicating the inadequacy of empiricist accounts of the self. However, Hume's problem can be solved by defining personal identity in terms of bodily identity, and the latter in terms of the resemblance and continuity of sense-contents. This account is borne out by the fact that, while it is not self-contradictory to refer to an individual as having survived memory loss, this is not the case with bodily annihilation. Believers in an after-life are not referring to the empirical self, but to the soul, a metaphysical entity, logically unconnected with the self. The position taken here differs from Hume's, as he thought of the self as an aggregate of sense-experiences, not as reducible to them: to talk of the self is to talk of sense-experiences.

This thoroughgoing phenomenalism, coupled with acceptance that sense-experiences are private to the single self, invites the response that, logically, it is a solipsistic position, offering no good reason for believing other people exist. But this is not a necessary consequence of our epistemology. It is not argued that the probability of other people's existence can be inferred from our own experiences. Analogy can be legitimately employed to establish the probable existence of something we have not experienced, if our experiencing it is conceivable; but this is not the case with other people, when it is assumed that we have no access to their experiences, making them metaphysical objects. In fact, the assumption that others' experiences are inaccessible is wrong. Just as material things and the self are defined in terms of their empirical manifestations, so are other people, in terms of bodily behaviour, and, ultimately, sense-contents. The hypothesis that others exist is verified by the appropriate series of sense-contents occurring. Further, the distinction between a conscious human being and a machine is that the first satisfies, but the second does not, an empirical test to determine the presence of consciousness. This is the solution to the philosophical problem of knowledge of other people: it is a matter of pointing out the way that a certain type of hypothesis can be empirically verified.

This phenomenalism is consistent with the belief that human beings communicate and inhabit a common world. It does not follow from the individual's experiences being private to himself that there is good reason for believing those of others are qualitatively different from ours, because the qualitative identity and difference of two people's sense-experiences are defined by the similarity and dissimilarity of their reactions to empirical tests. To decide whether two people have the same colour sense, we see whether they categorize colours in the same way. The content of others' sense-experiences have to be defined in terms of what we can observe ourselves. If their experiences are seen as essentially unobservable entities, the nature of which has to be inferred from their perceptible behaviour, even their existence becomes a metaphysical hypothesis. Instead, the contents, as well as the structure, of others' experiences, must be regarded as accessible: otherwise, no significant statements can be made about them. There is good reason to believe we understand others, and vice versa, because of the appropriate effects of our respective utterances. Thus, despite the private nature of individual experiences, we are entitled to hold that we inhabit a common world with others.

Chapter 8
Solutions of Outstanding Philosophical Disputes (pp. 144–70)

One of Ayer's purposes has been to establish that, as philosophy's function is to elucidate the consequences of linguistic usages, there is no justification for the existence of philosophical schools. Philosophy's concern is with purely logical questions, and when disputes occur it is because one party is guilty of error. Non-logical questions can be dismissed as metaphysical, or subjected to empirical enquiry. The three great philosophical issues, those between rationalists and empiricists, realists and idealists, and monists and pluralists, are now examined, to show that in each case both sides' theses are partly logical, partly metaphysical and partly empirical. The intention is not to vindicate a particular side, but to settle certain questions, which have long divided philosophers.

Rationalism and Empiricism (pp. 146–50)

Rationalists maintain the metaphysical doctrine that there is a suprasensible world, known by intellectual intuition, which alone is wholly real. This is a senseless doctrine, for no empirical observation is relevant to it. The rationalists are wrong to think that there are *a priori* propositions, referring to matters of fact, but so are empiricists, who hold that all significant propositions are empirical. There are necessarily valid *a priori* propositions, which are not, as the rationalists believe, speculative truths of reason, but tautologies. Thus, rejecting metaphysics does not involve denial that there are necessary truths. The positivists' criterion for distinguishing between a metaphysical utterance and a genuine synthetic proposition, that the latter be conclusively verifiable, must be rejected. No synthetic proposition can be more than highly probable. A weaker form of the verification principle is preferable: a proposition is genuinely factual if any empirical observations are relevant to its truth or falsehood. The positivist doctrine, that symbols, apart from logical constants, must stand for sense-contents, or be explicitly definable in terms of ones that do, must also be rejected: symbols can be legitimately used, if it can be indicated how the propositions they help to express may be empirically verified.

No specific empirical doctrines are necessarily accepted. Hume's epistemological views about the validity of general propositions of scientific law are, but not his view that all general hypotheses are generalizations from a number of observed instances. Scientists do not just wait for nature to instruct them; as rationalists maintain, they sometimes consider a scientific law's possibility before having the evidence to justify it, and use deductive reasoning to determine what, if their hypothesis is correct, they ought to experience. Theorizing is a creative activity, and the mind is active in acquiring knowledge. But, while what the rationalists say about the role of intuition in acquiring knowledge is probably true, it cannot be validated intuitively.

Realism and Idealism (pp. 150–61)

The realist-idealist controversy becomes metaphysical when the issue of an object's being real or ideal (as opposed to illusory) is seen as empirical. No possible observation can resolve it, as it concerns the fictitious issue of whether or not the object has completely undetectable properties. Berkeleyan idealists hold that a thing's being real, or existing, is equivalent to its being perceived, so it is self-contradictory to say it exists unperceived, while its being perceived entails its being mental, making everything that exists mental. Realists deny that the concept of reality can be analysed, so no sentence, referring to perceptions, is equivalent to saying a thing is real. What they deny is right, but not what they affirm.

Berkeley maintained that material things cannot exist unperceived, because they are no more than their sensible qualities, which it would be self-contradictory to say existed unsensed. But he did not reject the common sense view that objects exist when people are not perceiving them, holding that God could still perceive them, proving his existence. His reasoning is erroneous. Realists say he does not distinguish the object sensed from the act of consciousness aimed at it, and that it is not self-contradictory to say that the former exists independently of the act. But Berkeley was right that the ideas of sense-experience are the contents, not the objects, of sensation, and that a sensible quality cannot exist unsensed. His '*Esse est percipi*' is true of sense-contents: saying they exist is just saying they occur. But he was wrong about the relationship between material things and the sense-contents that constitute them. The latter are not parts of material things, as these are logical constructions from them. This is a linguistic proposition: that to say anything about a material thing is equivalent to saying something about sense-contents. A material thing can exist, without being experienced, if it can be experienced and is a permanent possibility of sensation. God's perceptions are not needed, while people can be said to exist in the same way that material things do: the individual's own existence, that of others and of material things are to be defined in terms of the hypothetical occurrence of sense-contents.

The immediate data of sense are not necessarily mental, nor are things just the sum of their sensible qualities: things are logical constructions out of sense-contents, and the terms 'physical' and 'mental' apply just to the former. The belief that sense-contents are mental comes from Descartes, who, believing his own existence could be derived from a thought, considered the mind to be a substance, wholly independent of the physical, and capable of experiencing only what belonged to itself. But this is a metaphysical view. Descartes' use of thought to indicate a single introspective sense-content means it is not mental in the usual usage; and, even if a conscious being's existence could be deduced from a single mental datum, this would not rule out that being's having direct causal and epistemological relations with material things. In fact, there are strong empirical grounds for rejecting the complete independence of mind and body. The argument from illusion is cited in support of the doctrine that we directly experience only what is mental: but all this proves is that sense-content is not related to material thing as part to whole.

Many non-Berkeleyan idealists hold that a thing's being real is equivalent to its being thought of, making it self-contradictory to maintain that a thing exists unthought of, or that a thought-of thing is unreal. However, just because judging something to exist entails its being thought of, this does not make it self-contradictory to hold that an unthought-of thing exists. The belief that what is thought of must necessarily be real derives from the erroneous assumption that a sentence like 'Unicorns are thought of' has the same logical form as 'Lions are killed'. But, unlike being killed, being thought of is not an attribute, so there is no self-contradiction in holding that things that are thought of do not actually exist. Further, even if there were equivalence between being real and being thought of, it would not justify the idealist view that everything that exists is mental.

Overview

It is not self-contradictory to hold that things exist unperceived, which raises the issue of whether realists are right that there is good reason to think they continue to exist when not perceived. What it means is that certain sense-contents would occur, under certain conditions. The fact that one perceives a table and other objects, has always done so, and has seen others doing so, is a good inductive basis for the generalization that, in these conditions, they are always perceptible, even when no one is actually doing so; and so for believing material things exist unperceived. There are also good inductive grounds for holding that things exist that have never actually been perceived.

Monism and Pluralism (pp. 161–70)

Monists believe that stating any fact about a thing is to state every fact about everything, such that any true proposition can be deduced from any other, from which it follows that any two sentences expressing true propositions are equivalent. As monists use 'truth' and 'reality' interchangeably, this leads to the metaphysical assertion that 'Reality is One'. Their paradoxical conclusions arise from a crucial false step in their argument: that all a thing's properties, including relational ones, are constitutive of its nature. 'Nature' is ambiguous in this context: it could mean that all a thing's properties are relevant to its behaviour, or that they are defining properties of it; but only from the second would it follow that every fact about a particular thing is logically deducible from every other. But to attribute to something a property that belongs to it by definition is to state a tautology, so if all a thing's properties are constitutive of its nature, the absurd result would be that no synthetic fact could be stated about it. This false view gains plausibility from the ambiguity of a sentence like: 'If this object lacked the properties which it has, it would not be what it is.' This could be an analytic proposition, stating that a thing cannot both have, and lack, a particular property; but this does not mean all its properties are defining ones. While it is self-contradictory to say there is no news in a newspaper, saying that it is not on the table is not. One problem is that a predicate, which with one descriptive phrase expresses an analytic proposition, may with another express a synthetic one, despite referring to the same object. 'The author of *Hamlet* wrote *Hamlet*' is analytic, but 'Shakespeare wrote *Hamlet*' is synthetic.

As well as every fact being logically contained in every other, monists also maintain that every event is causally connected with every other. But causality is not a logical relation. If it were, the contradictory of every true proposition, stating a causal connection, would be self-contradictory. But, as Hume showed, such propositions concern matters of fact and are synthetic; their validity cannot be established *a priori*. Further, as this view would make all data relevant to every scientific prediction, it would be impossible to make any. But many scientific predictions are successful, vindicating judgements that much data is irrelevant, and showing that the monist doctrine is wrong.

Revealing monism's errors is important, in order to uphold the unity of science and philosophy's unity with science, with which, unlike metaphysics, it does not compete, as its propositions are purely linguistic. The philosopher's role is to elucidate scientific theory, by defining its symbols. Philosophical elucidation of scientific symbols is needed, so that their real empirical content can be identified. Further, without science, philosophy is virtually empty. Analysis of everyday language will remove some metaphysics, but these problems will soon be solved. The philosopher's role is to clarify contemporary scientific concepts, but he must understand science to do so. It is helpful to distinguish between the speculative and logical aspects of science: philosophy must become the logic of science, with the philosopher making clear the logical relationship between scientific hypotheses, and defining the symbols that occur in them.

Glossary

A priori **proposition**. Proposition the truth of which is known before or independently of experience, and which holds (or is claimed to hold) irrespective of experience. See Analytic (of propositions) below.

Absolute (of the validity of ethical judgements). That actions or things are either good or bad, right or wrong, and (usually) that this is known by intuition, an immediate mental awareness or apprehension.

Aesthetics. That which relates to appreciation of beautiful objects.

After-life. Surviving, or being resurrected following, physical death, and (according to Christian teaching) living in a perfect relationship with God.

Aggregate of bare particulars. The view that the purpose of philosophical analysis is to break the objects in the universe down, until the process can go no further, and their simple, constituent parts are reached. Ayer points out (Chapter 2) that the universe contains many complex objects, which are more than the sum of their parts.

Agnostic. One who doubts/is uncertain about the existence of God.

Altruism. Attitude of unselfishly considering others, and putting their needs before one's own.

Ambiguous (symbol). A sign, the meaning of which is uncertain.

Analogy. Drawing a parallel between two things on the basis of similarities between them.

Analyses of non-ethical concepts. Ethical or moral systems do not only analyse/discuss ethical concepts, but also address other issues (such as matters of fact, definitions of non-ethical terms), which relate to ethical values/judgements.

Analysis. The philosophical activity of breaking complex objects of thought down, until their simple parts are reached. As Ayer

Glossary

acknowledges, this approach to philosophy is particularly associated with G. E. Moore.

Analytic (of propositions). One in which the concept of the subject contains the concept of predicate, so the predicate adds nothing to the subject. Such propositions are necessary and certain, because they say nothing about the empirical world.

Analytical activity (philosophy as). See Analysis above and Moore below.

Apodeictic certainty. That which can be proved and is certain.

Arguments to God's existence from religious experience. Attempts to prove God's existence, which argue from what is claimed to be an experience of God (what Ayer refers to as the claim to be 'immediately acquainted with God') to the existence of God as the source of the experience.

Aristotelian logic. Aristotle's system of logic, which Ayer discusses in Chapter 4.

Aristotle (384–322 BC). Greek philosopher, student of Plato and author of such books as the *De Interpretatione*, *The Nicomachean Ethics* and *Metaphysics*.

Artificial system of symbols. See Russell's theory of definite descriptions below.

Atheist. One who is convinced that there is no God.

Atomistic metaphysics. The metaphysical doctrine that the world consists of what Ayer terms 'bare particulars', such that the objects, formed out of them, are mere aggregates and no more than the sum of their parts. Ayer maintains (Chapter 2) that it is no part of philosophical analysis to uphold atomistic metaphysics: the world contains 'genuine wholes', which are more than the sum of their parts.

Attributive proposition. Propositions that attribute a property to somebody or something.

Author of this remark. F. H. Bradley. See below.

Author of *Waverley*. The novelist, Sir Walter Scott (1771–1832).

Axiom. A fundamental proposition (as in geometry), which is accepted as true, and from which inferences can be made.

Being. Here, what existence is/what it means to exist.

Bentham, Jeremy (1748–1832). British philosopher and founder of utilitarianism, social reformer and author of *An Introduction to the Principles of Morals and Legislation* and *A Fragment on Government*.

Berkeley, George (1685–1753). Irish philosopher and Anglican clergyman who became Bishop of Cloyne in 1734. Author of *An Essay towards a*

Glossary

New Theory of Vision, A Treatise concerning the Principles of Human Knowledge and *Three Dialogues between Hylas and Philonous.*

Berlin, Sir Isaiah (1909–97). Oxford academic, political philosopher and author of *Historical Inevitability* and *Two Concepts of Freedom.*

Books of Divinity. Books about God or religious matters.

Bradley, Francis Herbert (1846–1924). British idealist philosopher, and author of *Principles of Logic* and *Appearance and Reality.*

Carnap, Rudolf (1891–1970). Austrian philosopher and exponent of logical positivism, who was a professor at Prague, Chicago and Los Angeles. Author of *The Logical Structure of the World* and *Logical Foundations of Probability.*

Casuistry. Working out detailed ethical rules to cover specific situations and circumstances.

Categorical commands. The commands or imperatives of morality, which according to Kant (*Groundwork of the Metaphysics of Morals*) must be carried out for their own sake and not for some other purpose.

Causation. Causal relationships, the relation between two objects or events, such that when one is present, or occurs, it produces, or leads to, the other. See Chapter 2.

Cogito ergo sum. From Descartes' *Discourse on Method*, and usually translated as 'I think, therefore I am'. For Ayer's discussion of Descartes' philosophy, see Chapter 2.

Conclusively verifiable. The logical positivists' criterion for distinguishing between metaphysical utterances and genuine synthetic propositions, that the latter must be conclusively verifiable in experience. Ayer maintains (Chapters 1 and 8) that no synthetic proposition can be more than highly probable, and prefers a weakened form of the verification principle: a proposition is genuinely factual, if any empirical observations are relevant to its truth or falsehood.

Conflicting philosophical schools. Different groups of philosophers, who hold different and contradictory views, as with empiricists and rationalists.

Confutable by experience. That which experience can show to be wrong.

Conventions (linguistic). Linguistic rules that are generally followed.

Cosmological argument. One of the traditional arguments for the existence of God. In his *Summa Theologica*, St Thomas Aquinas (c. 1225–74) tries to argue (the 'five ways' or proofs) from God's effects (the world and how it exists) to God's existence.

Glossary

Criterion. A standard for determining something.

Deduce. To argue from certain premises to conclusions from which they (may) follow necessarily.

Deductive system. A system of first or fundamental principles or premises, which, together with the conclusions deduced from them, would give a complete picture of reality. Ayer (Chapter 2) regards such an enterprise as metaphysical, unachievable, and not part of philosophy's role.

Defined ostensively. Define by showing, or pointing out, the object, instead of giving a verbal definition of it.

Definiendum. The word or symbol to be defined.

Definition in use. Not a synonym for a word/symbol or phrase (explicit definition), but a translation of the sentence(s) in which it occurs into an equivalent sentence(s), which does not contain the word to be defined or any of its synonyms. See Chapter 3.

Definitions of ethical terms. The meaning (and use) of ethical terms such as 'right' and 'good'.

Demonstrative symbol. Sign pointing to the actual existence of an object.

Demonstratively certain. Can be proved conclusively.

Descartes, René (1596–1650). French rationalist philosopher and mathematician, and author of *Meditations on First Philosophy*, *Discourse on Method* and *The Principles of Philosophy*.

Descriptive ethical symbol. Use of an ethical symbol, such as 'right' or 'wrong', to describe or state, not express (an individual's or society's), approval or disapproval of an action.

Dogma. Belief accepted on authority, and which may be held despite lack of supporting evidence, or even if there is evidence that it is not true.

Duty. That which the law, or a set of moral principles, requires/obliges us to do.

Egotism. Selfishness.

Einstein, Albert (1879–1955). German physicist and professor at Princeton, who discovered the theory of relativity.

Elliptical ways. Ways that contain ellipses, and so omit something.

Emotive function. The function of ethical language in expressing and/or arousing emotion(s). See Emotivism below.

Emotivism. The ethical theory, associated particularly with the American philosopher C. L. Stevenson (*Ethics and Language*), that the function and meaning of ethical terms, such as 'good' and 'right', and the

Glossary

propositions in which they appear, is to express or arouse emotions, not to state something that is true or false. See Chapter 6.

Empirical hypothesis. A theory or proposition, put forward as a starting-point for scientific enquiry or discussion, the truth or falsity of which can be determined by experience and observation.

Empirical world. The world that we learn about through our senses, and in relation to which we determine what is true or false on the basis of experience and observation.

Empiricism/empiricist. Philosophical doctrine that (sense) experience is the (principal) source of knowledge.

Empiricist. See Empiricism above.

English empiricism. The tradition of empiricist philosophy, particularly associated with Locke, Hume, Mill and Russell.

Entails. When the conclusion follows necessarily from the premises.

Epistemological/epistemology. See Theory of knowledge below.

Epistemological treatise. Book devoted to the subject of epistemology.

Esse est percipi. To be (exist) is to be perceived. See Chapter 8.

Ethics. Term generally used interchangeably with morality/moral; set of moral principles that tell us what is good or bad, right or wrong, the (philosophical) study of what is good and right.

Euclidean triangle. A plane triangle with three interior angles adding up to 180 degrees.

Eudaemonistic (eudaimonistic) moral theory. A moral theory, originating in Aristotle's *The Nicomachean Ethics*, which views happiness as the goal of ethics, and holds that it will be achieved through a way of life that combines rational activity and virtue.

Exhortations to moral virtue. Earnest urgings, addressed to others, to behave in a morally commendable way. Ayer points out (Chapter 6) that many ethical systems contain such exhortations, rather than confining themselves to analysis of ethical terms.

Existence is not a predicate. A point made by Kant, in his *Critique of Pure Reason*, that existence is not a concept of something that can be added to the concept of a particular person or thing. To say that a particular thing 'is' or 'exists' does not add a new predicate or attribute to it, but just affirms the existence of the person or thing with all its predicates or attributes. See Chapter 7.

Existential propositions (positive/negative). Propositions stating that something does or does not exist.

Experience. What relates to the empirical world, and the way human beings experience things. See Empiricism above.

Glossary

Experiential proposition. A proposition that records an actual or possible observation.

Explicit definition. A dictionary definition, one that gives a synonym for the word to be defined.

Faculty of intellectual intuition. Ability to have immediate intellectual awareness/apprehension of things (here, the metaphysician's claim to intuitive knowledge of facts that cannot be known from sense-experience).

First principles. A set of basic principles, from which, through the use of reason, a complete picture of reality can be deduced. Ayer rejects this approach. See also Rationalism below.

Formal logic. Science of inference or reasoning.

Formal relationship of classes. The use of logic to combine propositions into analytic ones, such that one can be deduced from another. See Chapter 4.

Formal truths. The truths of logic.

Generically different. Do not share the characteristics that are typical of a particular class of things.

Genuine whole. A complex whole, comprising interdependent parts (such as a human being or a computer), which has a value greater than the sum of its parts.

Genuinely cognitive state. A state in which there is genuine knowledge.

God of Christianity. The infinitely powerful and loving God, believed by Christians to have created the universe from nothing.

God's attributes. God's characteristics. Those of the Christian God include (infinite) power, knowledge, goodness and mercy.

God's nature. See God's attributes above.

Goya y Lucientes, Francisco José de (1746–1828). Spanish painter, whose works include *The Second of May, 1808* and *The Third of May, 1808* (showing the horrors of the Napoleonic War in Spain) and *The Family of Charles IV*.

Hedonistic moral theory. The philosophical view that pleasure is the main or only thing that is good.

Heidegger, Martin (1889–1976). German existentialist philosopher and Nazi supporter, and professor at Marburg and Freiburg, whose books include *Being and Time, An Introduction to Metaphysics* and *Identity and Difference*.

Hobbes, Thomas (1588–1679). English philosopher, mathematician and secretary/tutor to the Cavendish family (Earls of Devonshire), whose books include the *Elements of Law, Human Nature* and *Leviathan.*

Homogeneous. Of the same kind.

Hume, David (1711–76). British empiricist philosopher, who was a source of inspiration to Ayer. His works include *A Treatise of Human Nature, An Enquiry Concerning Human Understanding* and *Dialogues Concerning Natural Religion.*

Hypotheses of science. Theories put forward as a starting-point for scientific enquiry, which can then be tested empirically.

Hypothesis. A theory put forward as a basis for reasoning, or starting-point for discussion.

Idea. The term used by Berkeley and other philosophers to refer to anything, which is immediately known, such as sense-contents.

Idealist. Philosopher who holds that reality is, in some sense, mental/ in the mind. See Chapter 8.

Identity. See Law of identity below.

Induction/inductive. Inferring general principles or propositions from particular instances; inferring probable conclusions from premises based on experience.

Inductive generalizations. Generalizations that are the outcome of the most common form of reasoning, which infers probable conclusions from premises based on experience.

Infer. Concluding one thing from something else.

Intellectual intuition/intuition(s). See Faculty of intellectual intuition above.

Intelligible notion. Idea that can be understood.

Intransitive verb. A verb that does not take a direct object.

Intrinsic/intrinsically. In itself, that which belongs to a person or thing's nature.

Irreducibility. When one thing cannot be reduced to, or expressed in terms of, something else.

Judgements of value. Ethical and aesthetic judgements. Ayer denies (Chapter 6) that such judgements can be true or false. See also Emotivism above.

Kant, Immanuel (1724–1804). German philosopher and professor at Königsberg, whose writings (they include *Critique of Pure Reason, Critique of Practical Reason, Groundwork of the Metaphysics of Morals* and *Religion within the Boundaries of Mere Reason*) cover metaphysics, moral philosophy and the philosophy of religion.

Kantian moral theory. In his *Groundwork of the Metaphysics of Morals,*

Glossary

Kant expounds a deontological system of morals, which treats certain actions as being right or wrong in themselves, and not because of their consequences. Although morality is completely independent of God, as moral laws must be obeyed for their own sake, Kant argues (*Critique of Practical Reason*) that God needs to be postulated, if obedience to the moral law is to be rewarded with happiness.

Law of excluded middle. This states that 'everything is either x or not-x': for example, 'something is either a chair or not a chair'.

Law of identity. This states that 'x is x' and not something else (here x stands for any entity): for example, 'a chair is a chair', not a table, a cupboard or anything else.

Law of non-contradiction. This states that 'nothing can be both x and not-x': for example, 'nothing can be both a chair and not a chair'.

Laws of nature. Natural laws. These are generalizations, based on experience, and so it is logically possible that (if nature changes) they may be confuted by experience.

Laws of thought. The three basic logical principles, the laws of identity, non-contradiction and excluded middle (see above), enunciated by Aristotle.

Literal significance. A proposition has literal significance if it is a tautology (analytically true), or capable of being empirically verified.

Locke, John (1632–1704). English empiricist philosopher, medical practitioner and administrator, whose works include *An Essay Concerning Human Understanding*, *Two Treatises of Government* and *The Reasonableness of Christianity*.

Logic. Science of inference or reasoning.

Logical constants. Terms in logical systems that have fixed meanings.

Logical construction. Something that is defined logically (according to the rules of logic) in terms of something else, as a material object is in terms of sense-contents.

Logical positivist(s). A philosopher who uses the criterion of conclusive verifiability (see above) to distinguish between metaphysical utterances and genuine synthetic propositions.

Logically certain. That which is necessarily true, denial of which involves a self-contradiction.

Material substratum. The underlying substance or 'something' of which material things are made.

Maxims of common sense. Common sense rules or principles.

Metaethics. Study of the nature of moral argument and the meaning and use of such moral terms as 'good' and 'right'.

Metaphysical/metaphysician/metaphysics. Originally (related to) the study of what is after (beyond) physics, and so the investigation of what really exists, of ultimate reality. Ayer uses the terms disparagingly, to describe those philosophers who believe that philosophy can provide knowledge of a reality that transcends the world of science and common sense. Metaphysical propositions are neither analytical truths of logic or mathematics, nor are they capable of being empirically verified.

Metaphysical notion of substance. The idea that the universe consists of one (or more) fundamental substance(s).

Metaphysical pseudo-proposition. A sentence that is neither analytically true, nor capable of being empirically verified.

Mill, John Stuart (1806–73). Utilitarian and empiricist philosopher, social reformer, East India Company administrator and MP, whose writings include *A System of Logic, An Examination of Sir William Hamilton's Philosophy, Utilitarianism, On Liberty* and *The Subjection of Women.*

Modified verification principle. To expresses a genuine empirical hypothesis, a sentence need not be conclusively verifiable, but a possible sense-experience must be relevant to determining its truth or falsehood.

Monist. A philosopher who holds that reality is made up of one fundamental substance.

Moore, George Edward (1873–1958). British analytical and moral philosopher, who was professor of philosophy at Cambridge, and whose books include *Principia Ethica, Ethics,* and *Some Main Problems of Philosophy.*

Moral philosophy. Branch of philosophy concerned with moral issues and the general principles of morality. Ayer argues (Chapter 6) that it should be confined to analysis of ethical terms (see Metaethics above).

Moral precepts. Moral rules or principles.

Moral sanctions. Penalties designed to secure obedience to moral rules.

Moral sentiments. Moral feelings, feelings about what is right or wrong.

Mystical. That which arises from a spiritual or supernatural source.

Natural phenomena. Natural things/events that can be perceived by the senses.

Naturalistic fallacy. In his *Principia Ethica*, Moore calls the fallacy of confusing good with/defining it as a natural property or object, such as pleasure, the 'naturalistic fallacy'.

Glossary

Naturalistic theories (of ethics). Theories that define what is good or right in terms of such natural properties as pleasure/happiness or what the majority approves.

Necessary (of propositions). One that must be true, because its denial would involve a contradiction.

Necessary and sufficient condition. A condition that is indispensable to, and sufficient to bring about/achieve, something.

Necessary truths. See Necessary (of propositions) above.

Negative existential sentence. See Existential propositions (positive/negative) above.

Non-animistic religion. Religion that does not locate its god(s) or supernatural beings in physical objects, such as trees or stones, but believes that it/they transcend the empirical world.

Non-contradiction. See Law of non-contradiction above.

Non-empirical world of values. A system of values, which is above or outside the empirical world, and which cannot be known by empirical means. For example, Plato held that there is an intelligible world (one that can only be known about by the mind), within which the form of the good has the same relation to intelligible objects as the sun has to visible objects in the visible world, and which is the source of reality, truth and goodness.

Non-Euclidean geometries. The *Elements* of the Greek mathematician Euclid (c. 300 BC), was the accepted authority on plane geometry, until the appearance of non-Euclidean geometry in the nineteenth century.

Nonsense. That which is not capable of being verified empirically.

Normative ethical symbols. Ethical terms that indicate judgements of value or prescribe rules for conduct.

Nothing. Ayer argues (Chapter 1) that the view that there must be a real entity, corresponding to a word or phrase that can be the subject of a sentence, leads philosophers like Heidegger to maintain that there must be something, to which 'Nothing' refers.

Ontological argument. In his *Proslogion*, St Anselm (1033–1109) tries to argue from the concept of God (as a being than which none greater can be thought) to his existence.

Ostensive. See Defined ostensively above.

Phenomena of moral experience and their causes. Manifestations of moral activity (moral beliefs/values and the conduct that results from them) and their causes.

Phenomenal world. Empirical world, the world of the senses.

Phenomenalism. The philosophical view that the external world/

material things are to be understood and expressed in terms of actual and possible sense experiences. Ayer refers (Chapter 8) to Mill's definition of a material thing as 'a permanent possibility of sensation'.

Philosopher. One who studies and practises/teaches philosophy.

Philosophy. Literally, love of wisdom, which involves the study of ultimate reality, what really exists, the most general principles of things. However, in *Language, Truth and Logic*, Ayer argues that metaphysics is no part of philosophy, which should become the logic of science, clarifying and defining the logical relationship between scientific hypotheses and the symbols used in them. See Chapter 8.

Plato (c. 429–347 BC). Greek philosopher, who was a student of Socrates, and who taught Aristotle at his Academy (the world's first university) in Athens. His writings include *The Republic, Theaetetus, Symposium, Phaedrus* and *Laws*.

Pluralist. A philosopher who holds that reality is not one substance, but many.

Poincaré, Jules Henri (1854–1912). French logician, mathematician and philosopher of science, whose works include *Science and Hypothesis* and *Mathematics and Science: Last Essays*.

Positivist. See Logical positivist above.

Postulate. That which needs to be assumed as a basis for reasoning, in order to make sense of something.

Practical verifiability. Where a proposition can be verified in practice.

Pragmatically. On practical grounds, on the basis of its results.

Premise. One of the propositions in an argument, on the basis of which the conclusion is reached.

Principle of inference. A rule that enables us to draw an inference. See Chapter 4.

Probable. What is more/most likely.

Problem of induction. The problem of identifying a means of proving that empirical generalizations, based on past experience, will continue to apply in the future. See Chapter 2.

Problem of perception. The problem of the relationship between sense-contents and the physical objects, which (it is believed) give rise to them, and how sentences about the latter can be translated into sentences about the former. See Chapter 3.

Proposition. A statement, which may or may not be true. See also Analytic above and Synthetic below.

Propositional calculus. See Formal relationship of classes above.

Glossary

Pseudo-concept. What appears to be, but is not, a concept.

Psychology and psycho-analysis. Scientific study of the human mind and (generally) the use of psychological knowledge in treatment of mental disorders.

Purely mystical intuition. Wholly supernatural or spiritual apprehension. Ayer argues (Chapter 6) that if this is how God is known about, he cannot be defined in terms that are intelligible to the reason.

Putative statement of fact. What is supposed to be/regarded as being a statement of fact.

Qualitative similarity. Alike in terms of their quality: as between our sense-contents and those of other living bodies.

Questions of value. Issues of whether things or actions are better or worse ethically or aesthetically. Ayer argues (Chapter 6) that there is no such thing as ethical or aesthetic knowledge, and that judgements of value are not synthetic propositions, but expressions of emotion.

Rationalism/rationalist. Philosophical doctrine that reason, rather than (sense) experience is the (principal) source of knowledge.

Realist. Philosopher who holds that reality is not in the mind, and that the external world/material things really exist. See Chapter 8.

Reality is One. See Monist above.

Reduction (of sentences about material things into ones about sense-contents). See Phenomenalism above.

Regularity in nature amounts to sufficient evidence for God's existence. That the order in nature (that the world is a stable environment, which operates in an orderly and predictable way) is proof that it was designed by an intelligent being: God.

Relation of equivalence. A way of saying that two sentences have the same meaning, without using the word 'meaning', as it can signify that the sentences affect people's thoughts in the same way (see Chapter 3).

Relations are not particulars, but universals. That relations, such as 'in', 'before', 'between', are universals, in the same way as properties or qualities, such as 'whiteness' or 'triangularity', where particular instances will have the property or quality in common.

Relations of ideas. The *a priori* propositions of logic and pure mathematics, which are necessary and certain, because they are analytic and say nothing about the empirical world.

Relation-symbols. Words/conventional signs standing for relations, such as 'in', 'between', 'before'.

Resemblant. Resemble each other.

Glossary

Russell, Bertrand Arthur William, Third Earl Russell (1872–1970). British philosopher, mathematician, writer and peace campaigner, whose writings include *Principia Mathematica*, *The Problems of Philosophy* and *History of Western Philosophy*.

Russell's theory of definite descriptions. Russell's theory that states that a sentence(s) containing a definite descriptive word/symbol or phrase can be translated into one(s) that does not contain that expression, but which does have a sub-sentence, asserting that one, and only one, object possesses a certain property, or that no object possesses it. For example, 'the round square cannot exist' is equivalent to 'no one thing can be both square and round'. This makes it clear that there is no (special or metaphysical) sense in which a round square exists. See Chapter 3.

Ryle, Gilbert (1900–76). British philosopher and professor of philosophy at Oxford, who was Ayer's tutor at Oxford. His books include *The Concept of Mind*, *Dilemmas* and *Plato's Progress*.

Sceptic. One who doubts, doubts everything (Pyrrhonian or Cartesian doubt), or who refuses to accept non-empirical sources of knowledge.

Schlick, Moritz (1882–1936). German-born philosopher and logical positivist, professor of philosophy at the University of Vienna, and author of *General Theory of Knowledge* and *The Problems of Ethics*.

School metaphysics. Medieval metaphysics.

Self/empirical self. The nature of the self: whether there is a permanent self, or (as Hume argued) just a bundle of sensations. See Chapter 7.

Sensations. The direct perceptions of objects or emotions.

Sense-content(s). That which is given by the senses/is immediately known in sensation, such as colours, sounds, and so on, as opposed to the physical objects, which (it is believed) give rise to them.

Sense-data/datum. A more common term for what Ayer calls 'sense-contents'.

Sense-experience. That which is experienced through the senses (visual, tactual, and so on), and which consists of sense-contents.

Sense-field. That which is/is capable of being sensed at a given point.

Senseless. Not empirically verifiable.

Sensible form. The form in which they are accessible to the senses.

Sensible properties. The properties of a thing that are capable of being sensed.

Set of values. Set of ethical principles.

Glossary

Solipsistic position. Believing that oneself alone exists, arising from the view that one has access only to one's own experiences, not those of other people.

Sophisticated religions. Religions, such as Christianity, which believe in a God who transcends and controls the empirical world.

Soul/metaphysical entity. In Christianity, the spiritual element within human beings, which is the seat of personality and individual identity, which lives on after death, and which will be reunited with its body at the general resurrection. Ayer regards the claim that human beings have a soul as a metaphysical assertion that lacks factual content (it cannot be empirically verified). See Chapter 6.

Speculative knowledge. See Speculative truths below.

Speculative truths. Truths that come from speculation or conjecture. Ayer does not accept that the philosophy gives access to truths that are inaccessible to scientific enquiry, which uses empirical methods. See also Empiricism/empiricist and Rationalism/rationalist above.

Strong and weak senses of verifiability. The first is when the truth of a proposition can be conclusively verified in experience, the second is when there is the possibility of experience making it probable.

Subjective intension. What the individual mind or will conceives or intends.

Subjectivist (ethical). One defines the rightness of actions, and the goodness of ends, in terms of the feelings of approval they elicit. See Chapter 6.

Substance(s). The essence(s) of something/things, which makes it/them what it is/they are.

Substantival ego and its mysterious acts. That the individual self is to be identified with the mind, which is a pure, indivisible and imperishable substance, raising the question of how it interacts with the divisible and perishable body, in which it is located.

Super-empirical. Beyond/outside experience.

Suprasensible world. A world that is beyond/transcends the ordinary physical world that we know about through experience/the senses.

Symbol. Character that is the conventional sign for something else.

Symbol in use. See Symbol and Definition in use, above.

Symbolism. A system of symbols.

Synonym/synonymous. A word that has the same meaning as another.

Synthetic (of propositions). One in which the concept of the subject does not contain the concept of the predicate, but in which the predicate adds something to the subject.

Tactual. That which can be experienced through the sense of touch.

Glossary

Tautology. Saying something twice in different ways.

The Absolute enters into, but is itself incapable of, evolution and progress. A quotation from F. H. Bradley's *Appearance and Reality*, which Ayer cites as an example of a metaphysical pseudo-proposition (see above), which is not verifiable, even in principle.

Theorem. Statement in a branch of mathematics that requires a reasoned proof.

Theory of knowledge. Epistemology, theories about what human beings know, how they know what they (claim to) know and the limits of human knowledge.

Traditional logic. See Aristotelian logic above.

Transcendent God. A God, such as the Christian God, who is believed to be above or apart from the material or empirical world.

Uniformity of nature. The fact that the world is a stable environment, which operates in a predictable way.

Utilitarian(ism). A consequentialist moral system, which holds that acts are not right (or wrong) in themselves, but only to the extent that they promote pleasure/happiness and prevent pain.

Verifiability in principle. Where a proposition cannot be verified in practice, but it is known, in principle, what observations would be relevant to determining its truth or falsity.

Verifiable/verifiability. According to Ayer, a genuine proposition must be either a tautology, the truth of which can be discovered analytically, or an empirical hypothesis, the truth or falsity of which can be determined by an actual or possible sense-experience.

Verification principle. The logical positivists' principle that a genuine synthetic proposition must be conclusively verifiable in experience. See also Conclusively verifiable and Logical positivists above.

Vienna Circle. The group of logical positivist philosophers, led by Moritz Schlick, which met to discuss philosophical issues.

Vision. Here, gaining access to a synthetic truth in a non-empirical way. Ayer does not accept that this is possible.

Waismann, Friedrich (1896–1959). Austrian philosopher and logical positivist, who was a lecturer at Cambridge and Oxford. Author of *The Principles of Linguistic Philosophy* and *Introduction to Mathematical Thinking*.

Whitehead, Alfred North (1861–1947). British philosopher and mathematician, who taught philosophy at Cambridge, London and Harvard. Russell's supervisor at Cambridge, he was co-author with him of *Principia Mathematica*. His other books include *Enquiry Concerning the Principles of Natural Knowledge* and *Process and Reality*.

Glossary

Wittgenstein, Ludwig Josef Johan (1889–1951). Austrian-born exponent of analytical philosophy, who studied philosophy at Cambridge, where he became professor of philosophy. Author of *Tractatus Logico-Philosophicus* and (posthumously) *Philosophical Investigations*.